Book of Piety and Islamic Manners

THE BEGINNING
OF GUIDANCE

Book of Piety and Islamic Manners

THE BEGINNING OF GUIDANCE

Abu Hamid Al-Ghazali

1 2 3 4 5 6 7 8 9 10

All rights reserved. No part of this publication may be reproduced, stored in a retrieval system or transmitted in any form or by any means – electronic, mechanical, photocopying, recording or otherwise – without written permission from the publisher.

© Light Publishing 2022

Abu Hamid Al-Ghazali

Book of Piety and Islamic Manners:
The Beginning of Guidance

ISBN 978-1-915570-10-9

www.lightpublishing.co.uk

بسم الله الرحمن الرحيم

CONTENTS

I. INTRODUCTION	9
II. ACTS OF OBEDIENCE	15
1. Etiquettes of Waking up from Sleep	16
2. Etiquettes of Dressing	17
3. Etiquettes on Entering the Lavatory	17
4. Etiquettes of Ablution	18
5. Etiquettes of Washing (or Greater Ablution)	22
6. Etiquettes of Ablution with Sand (*Tayammum*)	23
7. Etiquettes of Going to the Mosque	24
8. Etiquettes of Entering the Mosque	25
9. Manners after Sunrise to Noon (*Zawal*)	31
A. Beneficial Knowledge	32
B. Worship	33
C. Good Deeds	34
D. Earning a *halal* living	34
10. Preparation for the other Acts of Worship	36
11. Going to Sleep	39
12. Etiquettes of *Salah*	42
13. Leading and Following in the Worship	47
14. Friday	48
15. Fasting	51

III. THE AVOIDANCE OF SINS 55
1. Lying 57
2. Breaking promises 57
3. Backbiting 58
4. Wrangling, arguing and disputing with people about matters of theology and metaphysics 59
5. Self-adulation 60
6. Cursing 61
7. Supplicating against people 61
8. Jesting, ridiculing and mocking others 62
9. The Sins of the Heart 66

IV. RELATIONSHIP BETWEEN GOD AND MAN, AND BETWEEN MAN AND MAN 75
1. Companionship with God 75
2. Companionship and Association with People 76
    A. Etiquettes of the scholar 76
    B. Etiquettes of the student 77
    C. Etiquettes of the child (with parent) 77
    D. Etiquettes with unknown people 78
    E. Etiquettes with friends 78
3. Association with acquaintances 84

I. INTRODUCTION

Praise be to God as is His right, and blessing and peace be upon the best of His creation, Muhammad, and his family and Companions after him.

With eager desire you are setting out to acquire knowledge, my friend; for yourself you are making clear how genuine is your longing and how passionate your thirst for it. Be sure that, if in your quest for knowledge your aim is to gain something for yourself and to surpass your fellows, to attract men's attention to yourself and to amass this worldly vanities, then you are racing to bring your religion to nothing and destroy yourself, to sell your eternal life for the present one; your bargain is dead loss, you are trading without profit. Your teacher abets you in your disobedience and is partner in your loss. He is like the one who sells a sword to a bandit, for in the words of the Prophet (peace be upon him), 'whoever aids and abets a sin, even by half word, is a partner in that sin'.

On the other hand, if in seeking knowledge your intention and purpose between God Most High and yourself is to receive guidance and not merely to acquire information, then rejoice. The angels will spread out their wings for you when you walk, and the fish of the sea will ask pardon from God for you when you press forward. Above all, however, you must realise that the guidance which is the fruit of knowledge has a beginning and an ending, an outward aspect and an inward. No one can reach the ending until he has completed the beginning; no one can discover the inward aspect until he has mastered the outward.

Here, then, I give you counsel about the Beginning of Guidance, so that thereby you may test yourself and examine your heart. If you find your heart drawn towards it and your soul docile and receptive, go ahead, make for the end, launch out into the oceans of knowledge. If, on the other hand, you find that when you turn to the matter seriously, your heart tends to procrastinate and actually to put off doing anything about it, then you may be sure that the part of your soul which is drawn to seek knowledge is the evil inclined irrational soul. It has been roused in obedience to Satan, the accursed, in order that he may lower you into the well by the rope of his deception, and by his deceit lure you to the abyss of destruction. His aim is to press his evil wares upon you in the place where good wares are sold, so that he may unite you with those 'who most lose their works, whose effort goes astray in this present life though they think they are doing well' (Quran 18:103-104). Moreover Satan, to impress you, rehearses the excellence of knowledge, the high rank of scholars and the narrations about knowledge from the Prophet and others. He thus diverts your attention from sayings of the Prophet (peace be upon him) such as the following:

- Whoever increases in knowledge and does not increase in guidance, only increases in distance from God; (Al-Daylami in al-Firdaws)
- The most severe punishment on the Day of Resurrection is that of the scholar to whom God gave no benefit from his knowledge; (Tabarani, Al-Baihaqi)
- O God, I take refuge with You from knowledge which does not benefit, from the heart which does not humble itself, from the act which is not lifted up to God, and from the prayer which is not heard; (Muslim, Al-Mustadrak)
- During my night-journey (mi'raj) I passed some groups

of people whose lips were cut by fiery scissors, and I said to them, 'Who are you?' And they replied, 'We used to command others to do good and yet ourselves did not do it, and to prohibit others from doing evil and yet ourselves did it'. (Ahmad)

Beware then, unfortunate man, of listening to his fair words, lest he lower you into the well by the rope of his deception. Woe to the ignorant man, when he has not learned even once, and woe to the learned man when he has not put into practice what he learned a thousand times!

People who seek knowledge are of three types:
1. There is the man who seeks knowledge to take it as his travelling provision for the life to come; he seeks thereby only the Countenance of God and the mansion of eternity; such a man is saved.
2. Then there is the man who seeks it for the help it gives in his transitory life in obtaining power, influence and wealth, and at the same time is aware of that ultimate truth and in his heart has some perception of the worthlessness of his condition and the vileness of his aim. Such a man is in jeopardy, for if his appointed term comes upon him suddenly before he repents, a bad end of life is to be feared for him and his fate will depend upon the will of God; yet, if he is given grace to repent before the arrival of the appointed term, and adds practice to theory, and makes up for the matters he has neglected, he will join the ranks of the saved, for 'the man who repents of sin is like the man who has none'.
3. A third man has been overcome by Satan. He has taken his knowledge as a means to increase his wealth, to boast of his influence and to pride himself on his vast following. By his knowledge he explores every avenue

which offers a prospect of realising what he hopes for from this world. Moreover he believes in himself that he has an important place in God's eyes because with his dress and manner of speech he bears the brand and stamp of the scholar despite his mad desire of this world both openly and in secret.

Such men will perish, being stupid and easily deceived, for there is no hope of their repentance since they fancy that they are acting well. They are unmindful of the words of God most high, 'O you who have believed, why do you say what you do not do?' (Quran 61:2). To them may be applied the saying of the Messenger of God (peace be upon him), 'It is other than Dajjal (or Antichrist) I fear more for you', and when someone asked him, 'Who is that?' he replied, 'An evil scholar'.

The point of this is that the aim of the Dajjal is to lead men astray. The scholar is similar. If he turns men from this world by what he says, yet he calls them to it by what he is and what he does. A man's conduct speaks more eloquently than his words. Human nature is more inclined to share in what is done than to follow what is said. The corruption caused by the acts of this misguided man is greater than the improvement affected by his words, for the ignorant man does not venture to set his desire on this world till the scholars have done so. Thus this man's knowledge has become a cause of God's servants venturing to disobey Him. Despite that his ignorant soul remains confident; it fills him with desire and hope, and urges him to expect a reward from God for his knowledge. It suggests to him that he is better than many of God's servants.

Be of the first group, then, O seeker of knowledge! Avoid being of the second group, for many a procrastinator is suddenly overtaken by his appointed term before repenting, and is lost. But beware, above all beware, of being in the third group and perishing utterly without any hope or expectation of salvation.

If, then, you ask, what is the Beginning of Guidance in order that I may test my soul thereby? Know that the beginning of guidance is outward piety (taqwa) and the end of guidance is inward piety (ihsan). Only through piety is anything really achieved; only the pious are guided. Piety designates carrying out the commands of God most high and turning aside from what He prohibits, and thus has two parts. In what follows I expound to you briefly the outward aspect of the science of piety in both its parts.

II. ACTS OF OBEDIENCE

THE COMMANDS of God most high prescribe obligatory acts and supererogatory acts. The obligatory act is the capital on which the trading activities are based and through which man comes to safety or salvation. The supererogatory act is the profit which lives a man a higher degree of success. The Prophet (peace be upon him) said: "God Most Blessed and Most High says, 'Nothing brings men near to Me like the performance of what I made obligatory for them; and through works of supererogation. My servant comes ever nearer to Me until I love him, and when I have bestowed My love on him, I become his hearing with which he hears, his sight with which he sees, his tongue with which he speaks, his hand with which he grasps, and his foot with which he walks.'".

You will never arrive at fulfilling the commands of God, my dear student, unless you watch over your heart and your action at each moment and at every breath from morning to light. God most high is aware of your secret being. He observes your inner and your outer being. He comprehends your every glance, your every thought, your every step, and whatever else you do, moving or resting. Alike in company and in solitude you live constantly in His presence throughout celestial and terrestrial regions nothing is at rest and nothing moves without the Lord of the heavens and the earth being aware of it. 'He knows the treachery of the eyes, and what is concealed in the hearts' (Quran 40:20); 'He knows the secret and what is still more hidden' (Quran 20:6).

So, unfortunate, your behaviour both inward and outward in the presence of God Most High must be that of a humble and erring slave in the presence of the powerful and victorious King. Let your endeavour be that your Master may not see you where He forbade you to be and may He not miss you where He commanded you to be. You will not manage to do this, however, unless you plan out your time and order your supplication (du'a) and litanies from morning to evening. From the moment you wake from sleep until the time when you return to your bed be diligent in performing the commands God Most High lays upon you.

1. Etiquettes of Waking up from Sleep

In waking from sleep endeavour to be awake before the start of fajr. Let the first activity of the heart and tongue be the mention of God Most High. Say here:

> 'All praises to God who gave us life after giving us death and back to Him is the resurrection; to Him are we raised up again. It is for God that we and all creation have come to this day. His is the greatness and the authority. His is the might and the power, Lord of the worlds. In the disposition of surrender to God (Islam) have we come to this day, and in the word of sincerity, in the religion of our Prophet Muhammad (peace be upon him). and in the community of our father Ibrahim, a hanif,[1] 'surrendered to God (Muslim), not one of the idolaters.

> 'God we ask You that You would direct us this day to all good. We seek refuge with You from committing any evil or that we should bring it to any Muslim or that anyone should bring it to us. O God by You we enter the morning, by You we enter the evening, by You we have life and by You we have death,

---

[1] One who rejected idolatry before Islam.

and to You is the return. We ask You for the good of this day and of what is in it; we take refuge with You from the evil of this day and of what is in it'.

2. Etiquettes of Dressing

When you put on your clothes make the intention of fulfilling the commands of God about covering your nakedness (awrah). Do not let your purpose in wearing clothes be to impress others, so that you go astray.

3. Etiquettes on Entering the Lavatory

When you go to the lavatory to relieve yourself, enter with he left foot first and come out with the right foot first. Do not take with you anything containing the name of God or of His messenger. Do not enter bare headed or bare footed. As you enter say:

> 'In the name of God; I take refuge with God from filth and defilement, from soiling impurity, from Satan the accursed'.

And as you leave say:

> 'Have mercy on me; praise God Who has removed from me what would harm me and has left in me what will benefit me'.

You must make ready the cleaning material (for cleansing) before relieving yourself, and you must not cleanse yourself with water from the place where you would relieve yourself. After you urinate you can cough and squeeze the organ three times for drops. Lightly extend the private organ three times by passing the left hand under it. If you are in the desert, go away from the eyes of observers, and keep behind some object if there is one. Do not expose yourself before you reach the place where you are to sit. Do not face in the direction of prayer, and do not turn either face or back to sun or moon. Do not pass water (urinate) in a place where people gather, nor in still water, nor under a tree with fruit, nor in a cave. Avoid hard ground and the direction of blowing wind so that you are not splashed at, for Muhammad (peace be upon him) said, 'All the punishment of the grave is from it.' (Tirmidhi) In sitting rest more upon your left foot. Do not urinate standing save in case of necessity. In cleansing yourself use both stone (modern equivalent would be toilet tissue) and water; if you want to use only one, water is preferable. When you have only stone, you must use three clean dry stones, wiping the anus with them in such a way that nothing else is soiled by the ordure. Similarly wipe the penis on three places of a stone. If it is not completely cleansed after three times, make up five or seven, so that the cleansing is completed after an odd number of times. The odd is preferable; cleansing is obligatory. Cleanse yourself only with the left hand. On finishing the process of cleansing say: 'O God, purify my heart from hypocrisy, and keep my privy parts from sin'. After completing the cleansing rub your hand on the earth or on a wall, then wash it.

4. Etiquettes of Ablution

After you have finished thus cleansing yourself, do not omit to use the tooth-stick (miswak). For that is a purification of the mouth, pleasing to the Lord, and displeasing to Satan. A prayer with clean teeth is better than seventy prayers without clean teeth. The following is related from Abu Hurairah (may God be pleased with him): The Messenger of God (peace be upon him) said, 'Were it not that I should distress my community, I would have ordered them to use the tooth-stick before every prayer'. There is also the following narration of the prophet (peace be upon him); 'I was commanded the use of the tooth-stick until I feared it would be decreed mandatory on me.'

Then sit for the ablution facing the direction of prayer (qibla) in a raised place so that the splashes do not reach you. Say:

> 'In the name of God, the Merciful, the Compassionate. 'O my Lord I take refuge in You, O my Lord, from their being present with me' (Quran 23:97-98).

Then wash your hands three times before placing them in the basin, and say:

> 'O God, I ask You for good fortune and blessing, and I seek refuge with You from misfortune and disaster.'

Then make the intention of removing the filth or of fulfilling the ceremonial preparations for prayer. The making of the intention must be omitted before the washing of face, for otherwise the ablution is invalid. Then take a handful of water from your mouth and rinse your mouth three times, making sure that the water reaches the back of it—unless you are fasting, in which case act gently—and say:

> 'O God, I am proposing to read Your book and to have Your name many times on my lips; through the steadfast word make me steadfast in this life and in the world to come.'

Then take a handful of water for your nose, draw it in three times and blow out the moisture in your nose; while drawing it in say:

> 'O God, make me breathe in the fragrance of Paradise, and may I be pleasing to You,' and while blowing it out, 'O God, I take refuge with You from the odours of Hell and from the evil abode'.

Then take a handful for your face, and with it wash from the beginning of the flattening of the forehead to the base of the chin up and down, and from ear to ear across. Make the water reach the place where water doesn't grow. It is the point from which women are accustomed to removing the hair and is what lies between the top of the ear and the corner of the temples, that is, the forehead aspect of the face.

Make the water reach the four places where hair grows: the eye-brows, the moustache, the eye-lashes and the sideburns; that is, what lies in front of the ears from the beginning of the beard. The water must also reach the roots of the hair of the thin part of the beard, not of the thick part. As you wash your face say:

> 'O God, brighten my face through Your light on the day when You brighten the faces of Your awliya (close friends), and do not darken my face with darkness on the day when You darken the faces of Your enemies'.

Do not omit wetting the thick part of the beard. Then wash your right hand, and after that the left, together with the elbow and half the upper arm; for the adornment in Paradise reaches to the places touched in ablution. As you wash your right hand say: 'O God, give me my book in my right hand and grant me an easy reckonings.[2] As you wash your left hand say: 'O God, I take refuge with Thee from being given my book in my left hand or behind my back'. Then, moistening your hands, rub all over your head, keeping the fingertips of right and left hands close together, placing them on the fore part of the head and moving them back to the nape of the neck and then forward again. Do this three times—and similarly with the other parts

---

2   At the Last Judgment, according to Islamic ideas, those who are to go to paradise receive their book, with the account of what they have done on earth, in their right hand; the others receive it in their left hand or from behind

of the body—and say: O God, cover me with Your mercy, send down Your blessing upon me, shelter me beneath the shade of Your throne on the day when there is no shade save Yours; O God, make my hair and my flesh forbidden to the Fire'.

Then rub your ears outside and inside with clean water; place your forefingers in your ear holes and rub the outside of your ears with the ball of your thumbs, and say: 'O God make me one of those who hear the word and follow the good in it; O God, make me hear the crier of Paradise along with the righteous in Paradise'. Then rub your neck, and say: 'O God, deliver my neck from the Fire; O God, I seek refuge with You from the chains and fetters.'

Then wash your right foot and after that the left, up to the ankles. With the little finger of your left hand wash between your toes, beginning with the little toe of your right foot and finishing with the little toe of your left; approach the toes from below; and say, 'O God, establish my feet on the straight path along with the feet of Your righteous servants.' Similarly when you wash the left, say: 'O God, I seek refuge with You that You may not cause my feet to slip from the bridge into the Fire on the day when the feet of the hypocrites and idolaters slip.' Bring the water half way up your legs. Be careful to repeat all your actions three times.

When you have completed the ablution, raise your eyes to the heaven and say: 'I bear witness that there is no god save God alone; He has no partner; and I bear witness that Muhammad is His servant and His messenger. Glory and praise be to You, O God; I bear witness that there is no god save You. I have done evil and my soul has done wrong; I seek pardon and I turn to You in penitence; pardon me and repent towards me, for You are the Forgiving, the Merciful. O God, make me one of the penitent, make me one of the pure, make me one of Thy righteous Servants, make me patient and graceful, make me remember You frequently, and I shall praise Thee early and late.'

If a man says these prayers during his ablution, his sins have departed from all parts of his body, a seal has been set upon his ablution, it has been raised to beneath the throne of God and it unceasingly praises and hallows God, while the reward of that ablution is recorded for him to the Day of Resurrection.

There are seven things to be avoided in your ablution.
- Do not shake your head so as to splash the water.
- Do not strike the water against your head and face noisily.
- Do not talk during the ablution.
- Do not repeat more than three times in washing.
- Do not, through mere scrupulosity, pour out more water than is necessary, for the scrupulous have a devil who plays with them, called the walhān (lit. 'distraught').
- Do not perform your ablution with water which has lain in the sun.
- Do not use copper vessels. These seven things are objectionable in ablutions.

There is a saying, 'If a man remembers God at his ablution, God purifies his whole body; if a man does not remember God, He purifies only those parts which the water reaches'.

5. Etiquettes of Washing (or Greater Ablution)
If you have entered the state of impurity from wet dreams or sexual intercourse, carry the container to the wash-place and wash your hands first of all three times, remove any defilement from your body, and perform the 'ablution before prayer' as prescribed above, together with all the prayers, postponing only the washing of the feet so as not to make the water unusable. When you have completed the ablution, pour water over your head three times, while making the intention of removing the defilement of impurity, then over the right side of your body three times, then over your left side three

times. Rub front and back of your body. Wet the hair of your head and beard. Make the water reach the curves of the body and the roots of the hair, both thin and thick. Avoid touching your private part after the ablution; if your hand comes in contact with it, repeat the ablution. In all of that in general the obligatory things are the intention, the removing of defilement (najasah) and the water to encompass the whole body. In the lesser ablution (wudu) what is obligatory, besides the intention, is the washing of face hands, including the elbows, and the washing of the Feet, including the ankles, the same number of times. The exact order and everything else are not obligatory but merely 'Sunnah Muakkadah',[3] which bring much merit and in excellent reward. The man who neglects them is the loser, nay more, he endangers his actual obligations, for the additional practices (nawāfil) force one to fulfil the obligatory ones.

6. Etiquettes of Ablution with Sand (Tayammum)

If you are unable to make use of water for various reasons;

1. There may be no water to be found although you have looked for it;
2. You may be excused through illness (from looking for it);
3. You may be prevented from reaching water by wild beasts or by imprisonment;
4. The water may be required to satisfy your own or your friends' thirst;
5. The water may be the property of someone who sells it at more than the proper price;
6. Or you may have a wound or sickness which makes you fear for your life. In one of these cases, wait until the time of the obligatory prayer comes;

Then look for some good ground with clean pure smooth

---

[3] Sunan mu'akkadah; prayer performed continuously by our Prophet

soil; strike it with your palms and grasp it with your fingers. Make the intention of fulfilling the obligation of preparation for the prayer;

1. Wipe your face with your hands, containing sand, once;
2. You are not required to make the sand reach the roots of your hair, either thick or thin.
3. Then take off your signet ring, strike the sand a second time with your fingers spread out, rub your hands including the elbows with the two handfuls of sand; if you do not go over the whole area with the first handfuls, take further handfuls until you have gone over it all. Next rub one of your palms with the other, and rub the spaces between your fingers. Now perform one obligatory prayer, and any acts you please of supererogatory prayer. If you want to perform a second obligatory Worship, make a second sand-ablution from the beginning.

7. Etiquettes of Going to the Mosque

When you have complied your purification, pray in your house the two rak'ahs of the Dawn Worship, should the dawn have already broken. This was what the Messenger of God (Peace be upon him) used to do. Then make your way to the mosque. Do not omit congregational prayer (jama'ah) especially in the morning. Congregational prayer (jama'ah) is seventeen times better than praying alone, If you are easy-going about a spiritual gain of this kind, what benefit will you have in seeking knowledge? The fruit of knowledge is only in its practice.

When you walk to the mosque, walk easily and calmly, and do not hurry. Say as you go: 'O God, by those who beseech You and by those who entreat You, and by this walk of mine to You, I swear to You that I set out neither lightheartedly nor heedlessly, neither from hypocrisy nor from desire to be well spoken of, but out of fear for Your anger and longing, to please You; I ask You to deliver me from the Fire and to forgive my sins, for there is none that forgives sins save You.

8. Etiquettes of Entering the Mosque

When you are about to enter the mosque, do so with your right foot first, and say: 'O God, bless Muhammad and the house of Muhammad and his Companions and give them peace; O God, forgive me my sins, and open to me the gates of Your mercy'.

Whenever you see in the mosque someone selling something, say: 'God make your trade unprofitable'. And when you see someone looking for their lost property, say: 'May God not let your property be restored to you — in accordance with the command of the Messenger of God (peace be upon him).

When you have entered the mosque, do not sit down until you have prayed the two rak'ahs of 'greeting prayer' (tahiya). If you are not ceremonially pure or do not want to purify yourself, the 'other good works'[4] three times will suffice, or, according to other authorities, four times, or, according to others, three for the man who is ceremonially pure and one for the man who has made the ablution. If you have not already performed the two rak'ahs of the dawn prayer (fajr), it is meritorious to execute them instead of the 'greeting prayer'.

When you have completed the two rak'ahs, make the intention of performing a private devotion, and use the same petitions as the Messenger of God (peace be upon him) did after the two rak'ahs of the dawn prayer.

Say:

'O God, I ask You for mercy from You to guide my heart, to settle my affairs, to order my disorder, to repel temptation, to reform my conduct, to preserve my secret thought, to raise up my visible act, to purify my works, to brighten my face, to inspire me to walk straight, to direct me aright, to satisfy all my needs, and to keep me from all evil. O God, I ask You for pure faith to fill my heart; O God, I ask You for true cer-

---

4 Such phrases as "Praise God', 'Glory be to God'; cp. Al-Baydāwī

tainty so that I may know that nothing will befall me except what You have written down for me, and for glad acceptance of what You have allotted to me. O God, I ask You for true and certain faith which no unbelief follows; and I ask You for mercy whereby I may receive the privilege of Your regard in this world and the next. O God, I ask You for patience with destiny, for salvation during the Day of Judgment, and for the ranks of the martyrs and the life of the blessed, for victory against enemies and the companionship of the prophets. O God, I come to You in my need; my thought is weak, I fall short in my actions, I am in dire need of Your mercy. I therefore ask You, O Judge of all things, O Healer of men's hearts, that, as You do rescue from the midst of the seas, You would rescue me from the punishment of the Fire, the torment of the grave and the trials of the grave, O God; and wherever my thought has been too weak, my actions too imperfect and my intention and desire too ineffective to be worthy of the good You have promised anyone from Your creation or goodness You have given anyone from Your worshippers, Indeed I pray and ask You for that goodness, O Lord of the Worlds. O God, make us to guide and to be guided aright, not to err and lead astray, at hostility with Your enemies and at peace with Your friends, loving men with Your love and hostile with Your hostility to those of Your creatures who have opposed You. O God, this is my prayer, but it is for You to answer; this is my utmost endeavour, but in You is my trust.'

And:

'To God we belong and to Him is our return; there is no power nor might save with God, the high and mighty. O God, of the faithful covenant and wise command, I beseech You to protect me on the Day of Judgement and to grant me Paradise in the Day of Eternity, along with the saints and martyrs who bow and prostrate themselves before You, and those who fulfil their covenant with You. Verily You are merciful and loving and do what You will. Praise be to Him Who is characterised by might and holds it. Praise be to Him Who is clothed and adorned with glory. Praise be to Him Who alone is to be praised. Praise Him for His grace and favour. Praise Him for His power and goodness. Praise Him Whose knowledge encompasses all things.

'O God, grant me light in my heart and light in my grave, light in my hearing and light in my seeing, light in my hair and light in my skin, light in my flesh and light in my blood and light in my bones, light before me, light behind me, light to right of me, light to left of me, light above me, light beneath me. O God, increase my light and give me the greatest light of all. Of Your mercy grant me light. O You most merciful'. When you have finished praying, let your occupation be only the performance of the obligatory Worship of meditation (dhikr) or adoration (tasbih) or reading of the Quran.

When, during this, you hear the call to prayer, stoy what you are doing and devote yourself to making the responses to the mu'adhdhin. When the mu'adhdhin says, God is great, God is great', repeat that, and similarly with all the phrases except 'Come to Worship! come to prosperity!' after these say, 'There is no power nor might save with God, the high and mighty'. And when he says, 'Worship is better than sleep', say, 'Thou hast spoken truly and well, and I bear witness to that'. When you hear the final call to prayer (iqamah), repeat what he says, except in the case of the phrase, 'The prayer is ready and established, at which say, 'May God establish it and continue it as long as the heavens and the earth continue'. When you have completed the responses to the mu'adhdhin, say: 'O God, I beseech You in the assembly of those who worship You and pray to You, at the retreat of Your night and the advance of Your day, that You would grant to Muhammad a place of favour and honour and an exalted degree, and raise him to the noble station which You have promised him, O You most merciful'.

If you hear the call to prayer (adhan) while you are yourself engaged in prayer, complete your prayer, then catch up with the responses after the greeting in the usual manner.

When the Imam commences the obligatory prayer (fard), do nothing but follow him in it, as will be explained to you in (the chapter on) the 'Manner and Conduct of Worship.' When you have finished say, 'O God, bless and preserve Muhammad and the house of Muhammad. O God, You are peace, and from You is peace, and to You peace returns. Greet us with peace, O Lord, and bring us into Your house, the house of peace. Blessed are You, O Lord of majesty and honour. Praise to my Lord, the high, the most high; there is no god save God alone; He has no partner; His is the kingdom and His is the praise; He makes alive and causes to die, yet He is ever living never dying. From His hand comes all our good, and He has power over all things. There is no god save God, the beneficent, the excellent, the praiseworthy. There is no god save God, and Him alone do we worship, serving Him in sincerity, though the infidels refuse'.

Then, after that, repeat the general comprehensive prayer (Jawami' al-Kawamil) which the Messenger of God (Peace be upon him; taught to ' A'ishah (may God be pleased with her), saying: 'O God, I beseech You to grant me all good things, both earlier and later, both those I know and those I do not know; I take refuge with You from all evil, both earlier and later, both what I know and what I do not know; I ask You to grant me Paradise and every word and deed, every intention and belief, that brings me near to it; I take refuge with You from Hell, and from every word and deed, every intention and belief, that brings me near to it. I ask You to grant me the good for which Your servant and messenger Muhammad (Peace be upon him) asked You; and I take refuge with You from the evil from which Your servant am messenger, Muhammad (Peace be upon him) took refuge with Thee. O God, whatever Thou hast ordained for me may its outcome be for my true well being.

Then repeat the words the Messenger of God (Peace be upon him) prescribed to Fatimah (may God be pleased with her), saying; 'O Living and Steadfast One, Lord of majesty and honour, there is no god save You; By your mercy I seek aid, from Your punishment protect me, leave me not to my own care one moment; make all my life upright, as You did for the righteous ones'.

Then repeat the words of Jesus (Peace be upon our Prophet and him): 'O God, I have entered the morning and unable to repel what I loathe and to gain what I hope for; by Your hand has this morning come, not by the hand of any other; I this morning am obliged to do my work, and no needy man is in greater need than I am of You, while no rich man is less in need than You are of me. O God, let not my enemy rejoice over me, and let not my friend think evil of me; May I not come into misfortune in my religion. May this world not be the greatest of my worry nor the furthest extent of my knowledge. Let not him who has no mercy for me prevail over me by my sin'.

Then repeat any of the well-known prayers you think fit; for this purpose learn some of those we have given in the book on 'Prayers' of The Revival of the Religious Sciences (the ninth book of the first 'quarter').

Your time between the Worship and the rising of the ;un should be allotted to four tasks: (a) supplication and invocation; (b) acts of meditation (adhkar) and adoration (tasbih), repeated with a rosary; (c) the reading of the Quran; (d) reflection—reflect upon your own sins, misdeeds and shortcomings in the service of your Master and how you have exposed yourself to His painful punishment and great wrath. Order your time, arranging your occupations for the whole day, so that thereby you become aware of shortcomings that you had overlooked. Beware of exposing yourself during that day to the dire wrath of God. Make the intention of doing good towards all Muslims, and resolve that throughout the day you will occupy yourself only with obeying God most high. Go over in your heart all the different acts of obedience within your power, choose the noblest of them, and consider how to prepare the groundwork, so that you may be occupied with it. Do not omit reflection on the approach of your appointed term and the coming of death which cuts short all worldly actions (aml), so that matters pass from the sphere of choice, leaving only sighing and regret and prolonged self delusion.

Include the following ten sentences among your acts of meditation and adoration (tasbih):

(1) There is no god save God alone, He is without partner, His is the kingdom and His the praise, He makes to live and causes to die, yet He is ever living never dying; from His hand comes all good, and He has power over all things;

(2) There is no god save God, the King, the Truth, the Evident;

(3) There is no god save God alone, the Victorious, the Lord of the heavens and the earth and what is between them, the Almighty, the Forgiving;

(4) Glory be to God, praise be to God, there is no god save God. God is great, there is no power nor might save with God, the High, the Mighty

(5) Glorious and holy is the Lord of the angels and the spirit;

(6) glory be to God, praise and glory to God the Almighty;

(7) pardon me, God Almighty, save Whom there is no god, the Living, the Steadfast, I beseech You for repentance and pardon;

(8) O God, none withholds what You give and none gives what You withhold, none opposes what You ordained, good fortune does not benefit its possessor, apart from You;

(9) O God, bless and preserve Muhammad and the house of Muhammad and his companions;

(10) in the name of God, along with Whose name nothing harms either in earth or in heaven, He is the Hearing, the Knowing. Repeat each of these sentences on your beads either a hundred times or seventy times or ten times; the last is the lowest number which makes the total a hundred. Continue these acts of meditation, and do not speak before the rising of the sun. There is a hadith (i.e., saying of Muhammad) to the effect that '...this is more excellent than freeing eight slaves of the descendants of Ismail' (peace be upon him and our Prophet); this refers to the practice of such acts until sunrise uninterrupted by conversation.

9. Manners after Sunrise to Noon (Zawal)

When the sun has risen and is a spear's length up, perform two raka'ahs of prayer, that is, at the end of the period disliked for prayer—for prayer is disliked between the time of the obligatory dawn prayer and the time when the sun is up. Then, when the sun is high and about a quarter of the day has elapsed, perform the forenoon prayer (*dhuhr*), four, six, or eight raka'ahs in pairs; all these numbers have been handed down on the authority of the Messenger of God (peace be upon him), with the remark that 'this Worship is the best of all; if a man wants, let him perform a large number of rak`ahs, and if he wants, let him perform a small number'. Between sunrise and the time when the sun begins to decline there are no regular sunnah's (*ratibah*) that are performed. The time that is left over from them you can spend in four ways.

A. Beneficial Knowledge

The first and best way is to devote this time to seeking really beneficial knowledge as distinct from the superfluities with which people busy themselves and which they call knowledge. Really useful knowledge is that which makes you grow in the fear of God, in awareness of your own faults, and in knowledge of the service of your Lord; it decreases your desire for this world and increases your desire for the life to come; it opens your eyes to the defects in your conduct so that you guard against them; it makes you aware of the plots and deceptions of the devil, and how he deceives scholars of evil (*'ulamā*) until he exposes them to the hate and wrath of God the most high, in that they buy this world at the price of religion and make their knowledge a means of gaining wealth from the powers that be and of eating up (unjustly) the wealth of trust-endowments for the poor and orphans; all their thoughts throughout the day are directed to the quest of worldly influence and seeking higher ranking in the view of mankind which forces them to hypocrisy, to quarrelsomeness, to argumentativeness in matters of theology and metaphysics, to boastfulness.

On the other hand, our conception of useful knowledge is what we have already expounded in The Revival of the Religious Sciences. If you accept this conception, study it and practise it, then teach it and preach it. When a man knows these things and practises them, that man shall be called great in the kingdom of heaven, according to the testimony of Jesus (peace be upon him).[5]

---

[5] Cp. Mathew. 5,19; 'whosoever shall do and teach them (The commandments of the law). The same shall be called great in the kingdom of heaven'. Al- Ghazālī had read at least part of the New Testament,

When you have completed that, and have also completed the reform of yourself outwardly and inwardly, and you still have some time free, there is no harm if you preoccupy yourself with the knowledge of madhab of fiqh so as to know the secondary issues of worship, and adopting the middle path between disputes when they are engrossed in their passions and that too should be only after completing these duties of communal obligations (*fard kifayah*). If, however, because of its occupation with such studies, your soul calls upon you to abandon the acts of meditation (*adhkar*) and reading of the Quran described above, you may be sure that the accursed Devil has secretly infected your heart with a latent disease, the love of influence and wealth. Do not let yourself be deceived by that and become a laughing-stock for the Devil, who will bring you to destruction and then scoff at you. But, if you test your soul for a time with acts of Quran-reading and devotion without, laziness and finding them burdensome, and if rather it is clear that you long to attain to really useful knowledge and desire only the countenance of God most high and the mansion of the life to come, then that is better than superogatory acts of devotion (*nawafil*), provided the intention is sound. The important thing is soundness of intention. If the intention is not sound, it becomes the point where fools are deceived and men's feet slip.

B. Worship

The second way is where you are incapable of attaining to really useful knowledge but devote yourself to serving God by such activities as meditation, Quran-reading, adoration and public Worship. This is the level of those who are fervent and live a good life. By this second way also you will be successful (that is, find salvation).

---

and had attempted from the Gospels themselves to refute the doctrine of the Divinity of Christ

C. Good Deeds

The third way is to busy yourself with activities which benefit your fellow-Muslims and fill the hearts of believers with happiness, or which make it easier for good men to do good works; for example, serving the professors of God's law, and the mystics, and ministers of religion, and going about their errands; and exerting oneself in feeding the poor and unfortunate, and going about, for example, visiting the sick and escorting funerals. All that is more excellent than supererogatory acts of Worship, for these are acts of serving God which at the same time show kindness towards Muslims.

D. Earning a halal living

The fourth way, where you are incapable of the previous one, is to busy yourself with acquiring the necessities of life for yourself or for your family, in such a way that no Muslim suffers any harm from you nor has anything to fear from your tongue or your hand, and that your religion is upheld by your not committing any sin. If you live thus, you will reach the level of the people of God's right hand, even though you have failed to rise to the levels just described. This is the lowest level of those which are included in religion, beyond these are simply pastures for the devils. Therefore you should busy yourself with such things, for in God is your refuge from what destroys your religion or injures one of God's servants. This (destroying one's religion and harming the servants of God) is the grade of those who perish. So beware of belonging to this group.

In respect of his religion a man stands in one of three classes:

> (a) he may be 'safe' (or 'saved), namely, when he confines himself to performing the duties of set obligation and avoiding sin; or

(b) he may be 'above standard' (literally, 'making a profit'), namely, when of his own will he makes an offering and performs supererogatory acts; or

(c) he may be 'below standard' (literally, 'incurring a loss'), namely, when he falls short of what is incumbent upon him. If you cannot be 'above standard', at least endeavour to be 'safe', and beware, oh beware, of being 'below standard'.

In respect of other men, too, a man stands in one of three classes:

(a) with regard to them he may take the place of just and generous angels, namely, by exerting himself for their ends through compassion and the desire to fill their hearts with gladness; or

(b) with regard to other men he may occupy the position of animals and inanimate objects, namely, where they receive neither benefit nor harm from him; or

(c) with regard to them he may occupy the position of scorpions, snakes and harmful beasts of prey, from which men expect no good, while fearing the evil they may cause.

If you cannot reach the sphere of the angels, at least try not to fall from the level of animals and inanimate things to the ranks of the scorpions, snakes and beasts of prey. If your soul is content to come down from the highest heights (*illiyin*), at least do not let it be content to be hurled into the lowest depths. Perhaps you will be saved by the middle way where you have neither more nor less than what suffices.

Throughout the day you must not busy yourself except with matters which will benefit you in the next life or sustain you in this, matters which are indispensable and whose aid is indispensable in the next life or in this. If in mixing with your fellow men, you are unable to maintain your religion (perform your religious duties) and attain salvation, then solitude is preferable for you; so you must take to it, and find in it salvation and peace. If in solitude evil suggestions draw you away to what displeases God and you cannot subdue them by devotional practices, then you must sleep. That is the best state for you and for us all. If we are unable to gain by spoils of battle, we should at least be satisfied with our safety and protection. But how mean is the state of the man who saves his religion by making his life empty! For sleep is brother of death; it is the emptying of life and assimilation to inanimate things. Realise this and you shall be facilitated God willing.

10. Preparation for the other Acts of Worship

You must prepare before the sun begins to decline for the noon prayer (*dhuhr*). If you rise at night (for prayers) or were awake for some good purpose, then take your siesta before midday; it is an aid to night-rising, just as a meal immediately before sunrise is an aid to fasting (from sunrise to sunset). On the other hand, a siesta when you are not rising at night is like a daybreak meal when you are not fasting by day. Endeavour to wake up before the sun begin: to decline, perform the ablutions, go to the mosque, say the prayer of 'greeting' (*tahiya*) of the mosque, and await the mu'adhdhin and make the responses to him. Then stand up and perform the four rak'ahs following on sun-decline (*zawal*). The Messenger of God (Peace be upon him) used to elongate this prayer and to say, 'at this time the gates of heaven are open, and I like that a righteous action is raised up (to God's throne) for me. These four raka'ahs before the noon prayer (*dhuhr*) are a 'strongly emphasised sunnah' (*sunnah mu'akkadah*). According to a Tradition, whoever performs them and makes the bowing and prostrating well, is accompanied in his prayer by seventy thousand angels, who continue to ask pardon for him until night.

Then perform the obligatory noon prayer (*dhuhr*) along with the Imam, and after that perform two raka'ahs for that belongs to the fixed and established prayers (rawatib). From now until late-afternoon occupy yourself only with learning or study or the helping of a Muslim or the reading of the Quran, or exert yourself in procuring such necessities of life as will be of assistance to you in your religion.

Then perform four raka'ahs before the late-afternoon prayer (*asr*); that is an emphasised sunnah (*sunnah mu'akkadah*). The Messenger of God (peace be upon him) has said, 'May God have mercy on a man who performs four raka'ahs before the late-afternoon prayer (*asr*); so make an effort to receive what he (peace be upon him) prayed for.

After the late-afternoon prayer (*asr*) let your occupations be similar to those before it. You must not be slack in the ordering of your time, doing whatever one feels like at any moment. Rather you must keep a strict reckoning with yourself and regulate your occupations and activities throughout the night and day, having something fixed to occupy every hour, and neither doing anything outside its fixed time nor doing anything else in that time. In this way the blessing on your time will be evident. If, however, you are heedless and neglect yourself as the animals do, you will not know what to do each hour, so that most of your time will be used up fruitlessly and your life will have slipped from you. For your life is your capital or the basis of your trading, by it you may attain to the joy of the eternal mansion where God most high is near. Every breath you draw is a jewel of invaluable worth, which nothing can replace. Once it has passed, it cannot come back. Do not be like the poor deluded fools who delight every day at the increase of their wealth and the decrease of their days. What good is there increase of wealth while life is decreasing? Delight only in the increase of knowledge and of good works, for these are companions in the grave when your family and your wealth, your children and your comrades are all left behind. When the sun becomes yellow, try, before it actually sets, to return to the mosque. Busy yourself with adoration (*tasbih*) and confession of sin (literally, prayer for forgiveness). For this, like the period after sunrise, is an excellent time. God most high has said: 'Glorify and praise your Lord before the rising of the sun and before its setting' (Q. 20:130). Before the sun sets recite the verses: 'By the sun and its morning brightness... by the night when it veils it' (q. 91:1-4); and when two Surahs of taking refuge (112; 114). Do not let the sun sit while you are still engaged in seeking forgiveness.

When you hear the call to prayer (*adhan*), make the responses, saying after the mu'adhdhin: 'O God, at the Approach of Your night, at the assembling of Your worshippers and the voice of Your suppliants, I ask You to grant Muhammad a place of favour and merit and an exalted degree and to praise him to the noble station which You have promised him, for You are not unfaithful to Your Promise'. And the petition as before.

Then perform the obligatory sunset prayer (maghrib), after the responses to the mu'adhdhin and the second call to prayer (iqamah). After that perform two rak'ahs before speaking, as that is the 'regular emphasised sunnah' (*ratibah*) at the sunset prayer (maghrib). If you perform a further four raka'ahs, that is also sunnah. If you are able, make the intention of remaining in the mosque in 'retreat' (i'tikaf) until nightfall in worship. Much has come to us (in Quran and Traditions) about the virtues of such a practice. This worship is the mashi'ah or begging of the night, since it is the first in occurrence (Q. 73:6). This is the prayer of the repentant. The Messenger of God (peace be upon him) was asked about the word of the Most High: 'They withdraw themselves from their couches' '(Q. 32:18), he said. This is the prayer between sunset and nightfall; it removes all idle words of the beginning and ending of the day. When nightfall comes, perform four raka'ahs before the obligatory prayer, thus filling the time between the two calls to prayer (the call to prayer proper and the iqamah). There is great merit in this. A Tradition runs, 'Prayer between the call to prayer and the iqamah will not be unheard.

Then perform the obligatory Evening Worship, and after it two raka'ahs of the 'emphasised sunnah' (ratibah). In the course of the latter recite Surah al-Sajdah (Q. 32), and Tabarak 'Mulk' (Q. 25:1-2) or Surah Ya Sin (Q. 36) and Surah al-Dukhan (Q. 44). That was the practice of the Messenger of God according to tradition. After that perform four raka'ahs; it is reported that this has great merit. Following on that perform the odd prayer (*witr*), three raka'ahs with either two salutations or one. The Messenger of God (peace be upon him) used to recite in these two extra prayers the Surah 'Glorify the name of thy Lord, the Most High' (Q. 87), and 'Say, O you unbelievers' (Q. 109), and Surah al-Ikhlas (Q. 112), and the two Surahs of Taking Refuge (*mu'awidatain*) (Q. 113; 114). If you have decided to be up at night for prayer, postpone the odd prayer (witr), so that the witr may be your last prayer for the night. Then devote yourself to intellectual discourse or the reading of a book; do not give yourself up to light amusement. Let these pursuits just mentioned be your closing activities before going to sleep, for 'activities are judged by the closing ones'.[6]

11. Going to Sleep

When you want to go to sleep, lay out your bed pointing to Makkah, and sleep on your right side, the side on which the corpse reclines in the grave. Sleep is the similitude of death and waking of the resurrection. Perhaps God most high will take your spirit this night; so be prepared to meet Him by being in a condition of purity when you sleep. Have your will written and beneath your head. Repent of your faults, seek

---

[6] A phrase found in Tradition referring to man's life as a whole; cp al-Bukhārī

pardon, resolve not to return to your sin, and so sleep. Resolve to do good to all Muslims if God most high raises you up again. Remember that in like manner you will lie in the grave, completely alone; only your works will be with you, only the effort you have made will be rewarded.

Do not try to induce sleep by flattering the bed feathers so that your bed is soft and smooth; for sleep is the rejection of life except when to be awake is an affliction for you; in that case sleep is safer for you. Night and day are twenty-four hours; the amount of sleep you take altogether, by night or day, should not be more than eight hours. It is enough, supposing you live for sixty years, that you lose twenty of these years or a third of your life. As you go to bed make ready your toothbrush and washing things, and resolve to get up during the night (for prayer) or else to get up before dawn. Two raka'ahs in the middle of the night is one of the treasures of the righteous man. Try to multiply your treasures in preparation for the day you'll be poor, because the treasures of the world will be of no benefit after you die.

As you go to sleep say: 'In Your name, Lord, I place down my side and in Your name will I rise up; forgive my sins; O God, keep me from Your punishment on the day when You raise Your servants. O God, in Your name do I live and die; and with You, O God, do I take refuge from the evil wrought by evil things and from the evil of every beast You take by the forelock; verily my Lord is upon a straight path (Q. 11:59). O God, You are the first and before You there is nothing; You are the last and after You there is nothing; You are the outmost and above You there is nothing; You are the inmost and below You there is nothing. O God, You did create my soul, and You will bring it to death. In Your hand is its dying and its living. If You make it die, pardon it, and if You make it live, preserve it from sin, as You preserve Your righteous servants. O God, I beg You for pardon and health. Wake me, O God, in the hour most pleasing to You and use me in the works most pleasing to You, that You may bring me ever nearer to Yourself and remove me ever farther from Your anger. I beg You and do You grant, I seek forgiveness and do You forgive, I pray to You and do You answer'.

Then repeat the Throne Verse [Ayat al-Kursi] (Q. 2:256) and from 'The Messenger has believed' (Q. 2:285) to the end of the Surah, Surah Ikhlas (Q. 112), Surah al-Nas and al-Falaq (Q. 113; 114) and Surah al-Mulk (Q. 67). Let sleep come upon you while you are recollecting the name of God and are in purity. Whoever does this, lifts up his spirit to the Throne and he is written down as praying until he wakes up.

When you wake up, return to what I told you first of all, and continue in this routine for the rest of your life. If continuing this is burdensome to you, be patient in the same way as a sick man endures the bitter medicine waiting for the cure. Reflect upon the shortness of your life. If you were to live, for example to be a hundred, even that would be little compared with your residence in the mansion of the world to come, which is to all eternity. Consider how in the quest for this—would you endure hardship and humiliation for a month or a year since you hope that thereby you will have rest for twenty years, for example. How, then, do you not endure these things for a few days in the hope of having rest to complete eternity?

Do not cherish long hopes lest your actions become difficult but suppose that death is near and say to yourself, 'I shall endure the hardship today; perhaps I shall die tonight', and 'I shall be patient tonight; perhaps I shall die tomorrow', for death does not come upon us at a specified time or in a specified way or at a specified age but encounter with death is inevitable so preparation for death is better than preparation for this world. You know that you remain here for only a brief space-perhaps there remains but a single day of your allotted time, perhaps but a single breath. Imagine this in your heart every day and impose upon yourself patience in obeying God daily. If you imagine living another fifty years and you enforce upon your soul the obligation of patience in obeying God most high, your soul will break away and deem difficult to the nafs. However, if you do what I suggest, you will be delighted at the time of death; but if you procrastinate and compromise, death will come to you when you do not reckon on it and you will sigh unceasingly. When morning comes and the night-journey is over, people praise night-travel; when death comes, you learn the outcome; 'you shall surely know the news after a while' (Q. 33:98).

We have now given you guidance in the arrangement of the periods of your day, and turn to the manner and rules of the prayer and the fast, and the rules for the Imam as both leading and being led for the Friday assembly (*jumu'ah*).

12. Etiquettes of Salah

When you have completed the
1. purification of the body,
2. clothing and
3. place of worship from all ritual and physical impurity, and
4. have covered your privy parts from navel to knee,
5. set your face to the qiblah standing upright with feet apart, not touching one another.

Then recite 'Say, I take refuge with the Lord of men' (Q. 114) as a protection against shaytan the accursed. Make your heart attentive, emptying it of evil suggestions. Consider in front of Whom you stand and speak, and shrink from addressing your Lord with negligent heart and chest filled with whispers of the dunya and evil passions. God most high is aware of your innermost thoughts and sees your heart. God accepts your prayer only according to the measure of your humility, submissiveness, modesty and lowliness (*khushu*). Serve Him in your prayer as if you see Him, for, even if you do not see Him, yet He sees you.

If your heart is not attentive and your organs not at rest, this is because of your defective knowledge of the majesty of God most high. Imagine, then, that an upright man, one of the leading members of your family is watching you to learn the quality of your prayer: at that your heart will be attentive and your organs at rest. Next, turn back to your soul and say, 'O evil soul, are you not ashamed before your Creator and Patron? When you imagined that you were observed by a humble servant of His, who was able neither to benefit nor to harm you, your members were submissive and your prayer was good. Yet, though you know He observes you, you do not humble yourself before His greatness. Is He, the Most High, less in your eyes than one of His servants? How presumptuous and ignorant you are!'

Use such devices in the treatment of your heart, and perhaps it will accompany you attentively in your prayer. You are credited only with that part of your prayer which you perform with mindfulness. In the case of what is done negligently and inattentively you require rather to seek pardon and make atonement.

When your heart is attentive, do not omit the second call to prayer (*iqamah*) even if you are alone; if you expect other people to take part, make the call to prayer (adhān), then say the iqamah. When you have performed the iqamah, make the Intention, saying 'I perform for God most high the obligation of noon prayer' (dhuhr). Let that be present in your heart at your takbir, (i.e., saying of Allahu akbar, 'God is great') and do not let the intention pass from you before you complete the takbir.

At the takbir raise your hands, which up till now have been hanging loosely, to the level of your shoulders. The hands should be open and the fingers stretched out, but without any effort on your part either to keep the fingers together or to keep them apart. Raise your hands so that your thumbs are opposite

THE BEGINNING OF GUIDANCE

the lobes of your ears, the tips of your fingers opposite the tops of your ears, and your palms opposite your shoulders. When they are at rest in their place, say 'God is great'. Then let them drop gently. In raising and dropping the hands do not push them forward nor draw them back, and do not move them sideways to right or left.

When you have dropped them, raise them afresh to your chest. Give honour to the right hand by placing it over the left. Stretch the fingers of the right hand along the left forearm so that they grasp the left wrist. Then following the takbir, say: 'Truly God is great; His praises celebrate; magnify Him early and late'. Next recite 'I have set my face towards Him Who opened up the heavens and the earth, as a Hanif, not one of polytheists' . . . to the end of the following verse (i.e., Q. 6:70-80). Then say, 'I take refuge with God from Satan the accursed. Then recite the Fatihah (Q. 1) with special attention to its doubled letters[7], trying to make a difference between your enunciation of the letters ḍad in your Worship. Say 'Amin', but do not make it continuous with the concluding words of the Fatihah (Wa la ḍalin). Let your recitation be audible at the Morning, Sunset and Evening Worships—that is, at the first two raka'ahs—unless you are following a leader (*imam*). Let the 'Amin' be audible.

After the Fatihah at Morning Worship recite one from the long Sūrah of the division of the Quran called the Mufaṣṣal[8] at the sunset prayer (*maghrib*) one from the short Surah of that division, and at the Noon (dhuhr), Afternoon (asr) and Evening Prayers (isha) one from the medium Sūrah of it, as, for example, 'By the heaven decked with constellations' (Q. 85) and those similar in length.

When travelling, use at the morning prayer (*fajr*) Surah

---

7 Take this to refer to the assimilation of certain final letter to the initial letter of the following word; cp. Cleverly. Worship, P. 67.
8 Usually from Sūrahs 49 to the end; cp. Cleverly, worship, 68n.

al-Kafirun (Q. 109) and Sūrah al-Ikhlāṣ (Q. 112). Do not go straight on from the Sūrah to the takbīr of the bowing, but make a break between them long enough to say 'Glory to God'. As long as you are standing keep your eyes down and restrict your gaze at the place of prayer (prayer-mat); that helps to collect your thoughts and encourages alternativeness of heart. Be careful not to turn to right or left in your prayer.

Next say the takbir of the bowing (rukū), raise your hands as before, and prolong the takbīr to the end of the Bowing. Next place your palms on your knees straight; set your back and neck and head all in one line; keep your elbows away from your sides--- a woman, however, does not do this but keeps them close to her sides, and say 'Glory to my great Lord and praise!' if you are alone, to repeat this up to seven or ten times is good.

Then raise your head until you are standing upright, and raise your hands while saying 'May God hear him who praise Him'! when you are standing steadily, say, O' our Lord, Yours is the praise filling the heavens and the earth and whatever else. You will'. If you are at the obligatory morning prayer (*fajr*) recite the Qunūt in the second when you have stood upright after the bowing (ruku).

Next promise yourself saying the takbīr but not raising your hands. First place your knees on the ground, then your hands, then your forehead. Keep your elbows away from your sides and your stomach from your thoughts- a woman, however, does not do this. Place your hands on the ground opposite your shoulders, but do not lay your forearms on the ground. Say, 'Glory to my Lord, the Most High!' three times, or, if you are alone, seven or ten times.

Then rise from the prostration (sujūd) saying the takbīr until you are sitting upright with your left foot under you, while your right leg is erect, Place your hands on your thighs with the fingers outstretched, and say: 'Lord, forgive me, have mercy on me, provide for me, guide me, restore me, preserve me, pardon me!' Then prostrate yourself a second time in the same way, and sit upright to rest in every rak'ah not followed by witnessing (shahādah).

Next, stand, placing your hands on the ground but not moving one foot forward as you rise. Begin the takbir of rising towards the end of the Sitting for Rest, and prolong it until you are half-way up the standing position. This Sitting should be short and as it were snatched.

Perform the second raka'ah of the prayer like the first, repeating the Seeking for Refuge at the beginning. At the end of the second raka'ah sit for the first witnessing. As you do so, place the right hand on the right thigh with the fingers closed except the forefinger and thumb, which are left free. At the words 'save God', not at the words 'There is no god', point with your right forefinger. Place your left hand on your left thigh with fingers outstretched. In this witnessing sit on your left foot, as between the two prostrations (sujud). In the last witnessing, however, sit on your hip.

After the Blessing on the Prophet (peace be upon him) make the well-known Traditional Supplication; during this sit on your left hip, with your left foot going out from beneath you and your right leg erect. Then, when you have finished, say twice, once to each side, 'Peace be upon you and the mercy of God', turning so that your neighbour may see your cheek. Make the intention of withdrawing from the prayer and the intention of peace for the angels and Muslims on either side of you. This is the form taken by the prayer of a person by himself.

The pillars of the prayer are humility and recollectedness of heart, together with the recital of the Quran with understanding and the making of acts of adoration with understanding. Al-Hasan al-Basri (God most high have mercy on him) said, 'Every Worship at which the heart is not present is more likely to bring punishment than reward.' The Prophet (peace be upon him) said, 'A man may perform the prayer so that he is given credit for only a sixth or a tenth of it;' and 'a man receives credit only for that amount of his prayer which he understands.'

13. Leading and Following in the Worship

The leader (*imam*) must make the prayer light, or quick, not burdensome. Anas (may God be pleased with him) said, 'Never behind anyone did I perform a prayer that was so light and yet so complete as the prayer led by the Messenger of God (Peace be upon him).' The leader (*imam*) should not say the takbir until the mu'adhdhin has completed the second call to prayer (iqamah) and until the rows of worshippers are even. At each takbir the leader ought to raise his voice, but those who follow him raise the voice only enough for each to hear himself. The leader (*imam*) makes the intention of leading in order to gain credit for this act of leading; but, even if he does not make the intention, the prayer of the congregation is still valid, provided they make the intention of following him, and they gain credit for worshipping as followers. The leader should say secretly the Opening Supplication and the Seeking for Refuge, in the same way as the man by himself, but he should say the Fatiha and the Surah aloud on every occasion in the morning prayer (*fajr*), and in the first two (raka'ahs) of the sunset and evening prayers. The individual does the same. He (the leader) says aloud the word 'Amin' in the audible part of the prayer, and likewise the follower, making his saying of 'Amin' coincide with that of the leader, not come after it. Ile leader is silent a little at the end of the Fātiḥah in order to recollect himself. The follower recites the Fātiḥah audibly in this silence so that he may be able to listen to the leader's Recital of the Quran. The follower recites the Surah audibly only if he does not hear the voice of the leader. At the Bowing and the Prostration the leader does not say 'Glory be to God' more than three times; and at the first witnessing (*tashahud*) he adds nothing after the words 'O God, Praise Muhammad'. In the last two raka'ahs he limits himself to the Fātiḥah and does not make the Worship long for the congregation. His Supplication at the last witnessing is of the length of his witnessing and his blessing of the Messenger of God (peace be upon him). At the salutation the leader (*imam*) makes the intention of peace, for the congregation, and the congregation in saluting makes the intention of responding to him. After completing the Salutation the leader waits a little and faces the people. He does not turn, however, if there are women behind Him, so that they may depart first. No one of the congregation stands up until the leader stands. The leader goes off either to right or left, as he pleases, but to the right is preferable. The leader (*imam*) should not perform supplications (duas) for himself during the the Qunut of the morning prayer, but speaking aloud, say, 'O God, guide us', and the congregation says 'Amin'. He does not raise his hands here, since that is not established in Tradition. The follower recites the remainder of the Qunut, consisting of the words 'You pass judgement, but no judgement is passed upon You'. The follower does not stand alone, but enters the row of worshippers or else attracts others to himself. The follower should not precede or synchronize with the leader in his actions, but should be a little after him; he should not bend for the bowing (ruku) until the leader has come to the end of the bowing (*ruku*), and he should not bend for the prostration (*sujud*) so long as the leader's forehead has not touched the earth.

14. Friday

Friday is the Eid of the believers. It is an excellent day, ordained specially for this community by God (May He be magnified and glorified). In the course of it there is a

period, the exact time of which is unknown; and if any Muslim, making request to God most high for what he needs, chances to do so in this period, God grants his request. Prepare then for it (the Friday) on the Thursday by cleansing of the clothes, by many acts of praise and by asking forgiveness on Thursday evening, for that is an hour equal in merit to the (unknown) hour of the Friday. Make the intention of fasting on Friday, but do so on Saturday or Thursday as well, since there is a prohibition on fasting on Friday alone.

When the morning breaks, wash, since Friday washing is obligatory on every adult, that is, it is 'established', and 'confirmed'. Then adorn yourself in white clothes, for these are the most pleasing to God. Use the best perfume you have. Cleanse your body thoroughly by shaving, cutting your hair and nails, using the toothbrush, and practising other forms of cleanliness, as well as by employing fragrant perfumes. Then go early to the mosque, walking quietly and calmly. The Prophet (peace be upon him) has said: 'Whoever goes at the first hour, it is as if he sacrificed a camel; whoever goes at the second hour, it is as if he sacrificed a cow; whoever goes at the third hour, it is as if he sacrificed a ram; whoever goes at the fourth hour, it is as if he sacrificed a chicken; whoever goes at the fifth hour, it is as if he sacrificed an egg.' He said likewise: 'And when the leader (*imam*) comes out, the record books are rolled up, the pens are raised, and the angels gather together at the pulpit listening to the invocation of God (dhikr).' It is said that people will be in the nearness to seeing the face of God (on the day of Judgement) according to their earliness to the Jumu'ah prayer.

It is said that, in respect of nearness to the beholding of the face of God, people come in the order of their earliness for the Friday Observance.

When you have entered the mosque, make for the first (nearest) row. If the congregation has assembled, do not step between their shoulders and do not pass in front of them while they are praying. Place yourself near a wall or pillar so that people do not pass in front of you. Before sitting say the prayer of 'greeting' (tahiya). Best of all, however, is to perform four raka'ahs in each of which you recite Surah al-Ikhlas fifty times

(Q. 112). There is a Tradition to the effect that whoever does that will not die until he has seen, or, in a variant reading, has been shown his place in paradise. Do not omit the prayer of 'greeting' even if the leader is giving the address. It is a usage to recite in four raka'ahs Sūrah al-An'ām, al-Kahf, Ṭā Hā and Yā Sīn (Q. 6; 8; 20; 36); but, if you cannot manage these, then take Sūrah Ya Sin, al-Dukhān, al-Sajdah, and al-Mulk (Q. 36; 44; 32; 67). Do not omit the recitation of the last Surah on the night of Friday (Thursday evening), for in it is great merit. Whoever cannot do that well, should recite Surah al-Ikhlas (Q. 112) many times, and frequently repeat the blessing on the Messenger of God (Peace be upon him), especially on this day.

When the leader (*imam*) has come out to commence the prayer, break off your private prayer (upon the prophet) and conversation, and occupy yourself with responding to the mu'adhdhin, and then by listening to the address (khutbah) and taking it to heart. Do not speak at all during the address (*khutbah*). It is related in a tradition that 'whoever says "Hush"! to his neighbour while the leader (*imam*) is giving the address, has spoken idly, and whoever speaks idly has no Friday Observance (credited to him);' the point is that in saying 'Hush' he was speaking, whereas he ought to have checked the other man by a sign, not by a word.

Then follow the leader in the Worship as explained above. When you have finished and said the Salutation, before speaking recite al-Fātiḥah, Sūrah al-Ikhlāṣ, and Sūrah al-Falaq (Q. 113) and al-Nās (Q. 114)) each seven times. That keeps you safe from one Friday to the next, and is a protection for you against Satan.

After that say: 'O God, Who are rich and praiseworthy, Who created and restored to life, Who are merciful and loving, make me to abound in what is lawful in Your sight, in obedience to You and in grace from You, so that I turn from what is unlawful, from disobedience and from all other than You.

After the Friday Observance perform two raka'ahs, or else four or six in pairs. All this is traditionally related of the Messenger of God (Peace be upon him) in various circumstances. Then remain in the mosque until the sunset prayer (*maghrib*) or at least until the late-afternoon prayer (asr). Watch carefully for the 'excellent hour', for it may occur in any part of the day, and perhaps you will light upon it while making humble supplication to God. In the mosque do not go to the circles of people nor the circles of storytellers, instead attend gatherings of beneficial knowledge that is, the knowledge which increases your fear of God most high and decreases your desire for this world; ignorance is better for you than all knowledge which does not draw you away from this world towards the Next. Take refuge with God from knowledge which does not benefit you. Pray much at the rising, declining and setting of the sun during second call to prayer (iqamah), at the preacher's ascending of the pulpit, and at the rising of the congregation for the prayer; the likelihood is that the 'excellent hour' will be at one of these times. Endeavour on this day to give such alms (*sadaqah*) as you can manage, even if it is little. Divide your time between the Worship, fasting, almsgiving, reciting the Quran, recollection of God (*dhikr*), solitary devotions (i'tikhaf) and 'waiting for prayer' (ribat). Let this one day of the week be specially devoted to what pertains to the future life, and perhaps it will be an atonement for the rest of the week.

15. Fasting

You should not restrict yourself to fasting in Ramaḍān and omit the business of supererogatory works and of gaining the higher degrees in Paradise, so that you have regrets when you look at those who fast and see them in the very highest degrees, as if you were looking at a bright star far above you.

The excellent days—the traditions bear witness to their excellence and honour and to the generous reward for fasting on them—are the day of 'Arafat (or 9th Dhū al- Ḥijjah) for those not making the Pilgrimage, the day of 'Ashūrā (10th Muḥarram), the first ten days of the month. Dhū al-Ḥijjah and the first ten of Muharram, Rajah and Shatan. Excellent also is the fast of the sacred months, namely, Dhū al-Qa'dah, Dhū al-Ḥijjah Muḥarram, Rajab; of these one is by itself and three adjoining one another. These are the days in the course of the year.

In the course of the month the days of fasting are: the beginning, the midmost and the last, together with the white days (full moon), namely the 13th, 14th, and 15th; in the course of the week Monday, Thursday and Friday. The sins of the week are atoned for by fasting on Monday, Thursday, and Friday, and expiate the sins of the month by fasting on the first, midmost and last days of the month, and the sins of the year by fasting for the days and months mentioned above.

When you fast, do not imagine that fasting is merely abstaining from food, drink and matrimonial intercourse. The Prophet (Peace be upon him) has said: 'Many a one who fasts has nothing from his fasting save hunger and thirst.' Rather, perfect fasting consists in restraining all the body organs from what God most high disapproves. You must keep the eye from looking at things disapproved, the tongue from uttering what does not concern you, and the ear from listening to what God has forbidden—for the hearer shares the guilt of the speaker in cases of backbiting. Exercise the same restraint over all the members as over the stomach and genitals. A Tradition runs: 'Five things make 1. man break his fast, lying, backbiting, malicious gossip, the lustful glance and the false oath'. Muḥammad (Peace be upon him) said: 'Fasting is a shield, so on day of you fasting; let him avoid obscene speech, loose living and foolishness; and if anyone attacks him or insults him, let him say, 'I am fasting.'"

Then endeavour to break your fast with lawful food, and not to take an excessive amount, eating more than you normally eat at night because you are fasting by day; if you take the whole amount you usually take, there is no difference between eating it at one meal at night and eating it at two meals (one by day and one by night, as when one is not fasting). The aim in fasting is to oppose your appetites and to double your capacity for works of piety. If, then, you eat food equal to what has passed from you, you have thereby made up for what has passed from you, and there is no advantage in your fast, while in addition you find your stomach heavy. There is no vessel more hateful to God than a stomach full of lawful (*halal*) food. When then if what fills it is unlawful (*haram*)?

So when you have understood what it means to fast, do so as much as you can, for it is the foundation of devotional practices and the key of good works. The Messenger of God (Peace be upon him) said: 'God most high said, "Every good deed is rewarded by from ten to seven-hundred like deeds, except fasting, for that is Mine and I Myself reward it".' The Prophet (Peace be upon him) said, 'By Him in Whose hand is my soul, the smell of the mouth of one who fasts is found more fragrant by God than the scent of musk.' God (most high and glorified) says; 'Should one give up appetite and food and drink for My sake, then the fast is Mine, and I Myself reward it.' The Prophet (Peace be upon him) said: 'Paradise has a gate called al-Rayyān, the beautiful, by which none enters save those who fast.' This is a sufficient treatment of the duties which constitute the Beginning of Guidance. If you want a discussion of almsgiving (*zakat*) and the pilgrimage (*hajj*) or a fuller treatment of the prayer (*salah*) and fasting (*siyam*), you may consult what we have said in our work on The Revival of the Religious Sciences (*ihya ulum ad din*).

III. THE AVOIDANCE OF SINS

Religion (*din*) consists of two parts, the leaving of what is forbidden and doing acts of obedience. Of these the leaving of what is forbidden is harder, for the duties or acts of obedience (as described in Part I) are within the power of every one, but only the upright are able to relinquish the desires. For that reason the Prophet (Peace be upon him) said: 'The true flight or Hijrah is the flight from evil, and the real holy war or Jihād is the struggle against one's desires.'

You disobey or sin against God only through the parts of your body. Yet these are a gift to you from God and a trust before you. To employ God's gift in order to sin against Him is the height of ingratitude; to betray the trust which God committed to you is the height of rebellion. The parts of your body are your subjects; see to it, then, how you rule over them. 'Each of you is a shepherd, and each of you are responsible for their flock.

All the parts of your limbs will bear witness against you in the courts of the Resurrection, articulating well, that is, with eloquent tongue, declaring your faults before the chiefs of the creatures. God most high says (Q. 24:24): 'On a day when their tongues and hands and feet will bear witness against them for what they have been doing;' and also (Q. 36:65): 'Today We shall set a seal upon their mouths, and their hands will speak to Us, and their feet will testify what they have been piling up.' Then guard all your body, and especially the seven parts, for Hell has seven gates, to each of which is allotted a portion of the people of Hell.

To these gates are appointed only those who have sinned against God with these seven parts of the body, namely, the eye, the ear, the tongue, the stomach, the genitals, the hand, the foot.

The eye has been created for you solely in order that you may be guided by it in darkness, that you may be aided by it in respect of your needs, that by it you may behold the wonders of the realm of the earth and the heavens, and learn from the signs in them. Keep the eye from three things or four, from looking at women other than those you may lawfully look at or looking lustfully at a beautiful form, from looking at a Muslim with a contemptuous eye, scrutinising the hidden faults of a Muslim.

The ear you ought to keep from listening to heresy or slander or obscenity or vain conversation or recalling anyone's faults. The ear was created for you solely that you might hear the word of God most high and the Traditions of the Messenger of God (Peace be upon him) and the wisdom of His companions, and that, by gaining knowledge thereby, you might attain to the realm enduring and everlasting bliss. If you listen with your ear to anything ill. what is disapproved (by God), what was for you (in your favour) will become against you, and what would have been the cause of your success (or salvation) will be turned into the cause of your destruction. This is the greatest possible loss. Do not imagine that the sinfulness belongs only to the speaker and not to the hearer. Tradition says that 'the listener shares (the guilt of) the speaker, and is like him a slanderer'.

The tongue was created for you chiefly that you might frequently engage in the mention (dhikr) of God most high (in acts of adoration) and in the reciting of His book, that you might guide God's creation to His way, and that you might declare to God the religious (din) and secular (dunya) needs of which you are conscious. If you use it for some purpose other than that for which it was created, you deny the goodness of

God most high in giving it to you. It is the part of your body with most power over you and over the rest of creation. It is, above all, the slanders of the tongue which throw men into Hell on their noses. So gain the mastery over it to the utmost of your ability, lest it throw you to the bottom of Hell. There is a tradition that 'the man who speaks a word to make his friends laugh is thereby hurled into the pit of Hell for seventy years'. A Muslim met the death of a martyr in battle in the lifetime of the Messenger of God (peace be upon him) and someone said, 'May he enjoy Paradise', but Muhammad (peace be upon him) said: 'How do you know he is in Paradise? Perhaps he used to speak about what did not concern him and was selfish where it gained him nothing.

With regard to your tongue there are eight things to be guarded against:

1. Lying
Keep your tongue from lying, whether in earnest or in jest, do not accustom yourself to lying in jest, for it may lead one to lying in earnest. Lying is one of the sources of major sins, and, if you come to be known as a liar, your uprightness becomes worthless, your word is not accepted, and (men's) eyes scorn and despise you. If you want to know the foulness of lying for yourself, consider the lying of someone else and how you shun it and despise the man who lies and regard his communication as foul. Do the same with regard to all your own vices, for you do not realise the foulness of your vices from your own case, but from someone else's. What you hold bad in another man, others will undoubtedly hold bad in you. Do not therefore be complacent about that in yourself.

2. Breaking promises
Take care not to promise something and then fail to honour it. The good you do to people should rather be in deed without

any word. If you are forced to make a promise, take care not to break it, except you are incapable of fulfilling it out of necessity. To do so is one of the signs of hypocrisy and wickedness. Muḥammad (peace be upon him) said: 'There are three things, which if a man practices secretly, he is a hypocrite, even though he fasts and performs salah: if, when he relates something he lies; if, when he makes a promise, he breaks it; if, when he is given a trust, he betrays it'.

3. Backbiting

Backbiting within Islam (in respect of Muslims) is more serious than thirty adulteries; so it is reported in a narration (*hadith*). The meaning of backbiting is the mention of matters concerning a man which he would dislike, were he to hear them; the person who does this is a backbiter and wicked, even if what he says is true. Be careful to avoid the backbiting of devout but hypocritical persons, namely, by giving people to understand something without actually stating it, as when you say, 'May God make him a better man, seeing what he has done has harmed and grieved me;' so 'Let us ask God to make both us and him better.' This combines two evil things; firstly backbiting, for by it people come to understand; and secondly justification of oneself and praise of oneself for freedom from sin and for goodness. Now, if your aim in saying, 'May God make him better,' was to intercede for him, intercede for him in secret; if you are grieved because of him (that is, for his sake), then the sin of it is that you do not want to criticize him and make public his wickedness; but in making public your grief at his wickedness, you make a public assertion that he is wicked. Sufficient to keep you from backbiting is the word of God most high (Q. 49:12): 'Do not go behind each other's back; would any of you like to eat the flesh of his brother when he is dead? You loathe it.' Thus God compares you to one that eats carrion. How fitting that you should guard against this (backbiting)!

There is another thing which will keep you from backbiting the Muslims, if you reflect about in, namely, that you should examine yourself to see whether there is any open or hidden vice in you and whether you are committing a sin, secretly or publicly. If you find that this is so in your own case, you may be sure that the other man's inability to free himself from what you attribute to him is similar to your liability, and his excuse similar to your excuse. Just as you dislike being openly criticized and having your vices mentioned, so he dislikes that. If you veil him, God will veil your faults for you; if you criticize him openly, God will give sharp tongues of power over you to impair your reputation in this world, and in the world to come God will criticize you before all creatures on the Day of Resurrection. If, however, on examining your exterior and interior life, you do not come upon any vice or imperfection in it, either religious or secular, you may be sure that your ignorance of your vices is the worst kind of folly, and no vice is greater than folly. If God desired good for you, He would make you see your vices. To regard oneself with approval is the height of stupidity and ignorance. If, on the other hand, you are correct in your opinion, thank God for it (your condition) and do not corrupt it by malicious people and ruining their reputations, for that is the greatest of sins.

4. Wrangling, arguing and disputing with people about matters of theology and metaphysics

That involves injuring and disparaging the other party and exposing his ignorance, and likewise involves self-praise and self-justification on the grounds of having superior intelligence and knowledge. Moreover it disturbs one's life, since when you contend with someone who is a fool he annoys you, and when you contend with an intelligent person he hates and feels animosity towards you. The Prophet (peace be upon him) said: 'If a man avoids disputing when he is in the wrong, God builds for him a mansion in the middle part of Paradise; if a man avoids disputing when he is in the right, God builds for him a mansion in the highest part of Paradise.' The devil must not deceive you by saying to you, 'Make the truth evident, without compromising'. The devil is always trying to entice fools to evil, presented in the guise of good. Do not become a laughing-stock for the Devil and have him scoff at you. To make truth evident is good when there is someone who receives it from you, that is, by way of counsel in private, not by way of debating. counsel (*nasiha*), however, has a distinctive form and character, and requires tact. Otherwise it becomes criticism, and produces more evil than good. If a man associates with the theologians (mutafaqqihah) of this age, disputation and argument come to dominate his nature, and it is difficult for him to be silent, since bad scholars have suggested to people that such things constitute excellence and that what deserves praise is the power to demonstrate and debate. Flee from them as from a lion. Assuredly, disputing is the cause of hatred with God and man.

5. Self-adulation

God most high says (Q. 53:33): 'So do not justify yourselves, He knows those who show piety'. When one of the sages (or philosophers) was asked, 'What is abhorrent and truthful?' he replied, 'A man's praise of himself.' So beware of falling into the habit of doing that. Such conduct assuredly lowers you in people's estimation, and leads you to hatred of you in God. If you want to appreciate the fact that praise of yourself does not raise you in other men's estimation, consider what happens when your acquaintances make much of their own virtue, influence and wealth. Your heart refuses to acknowledge what they claim, and your nature finds it excessive; when you have left their company, you blame them. Assuredly when you command yourself, they likewise condemn you in their hearts while you are present, and after you have left their company they manifest your faults when you depart.

6. Cursing

Beware of cursing anything that God most high has created, whether animal or food or man himself. Do not testify with certainty that a person of Qiblah (that is, any Muslim) guilty of polytheism, disbelief or hypocrisy. The one who is aware of inner secrets is God most high; do not interfere between God most high and His servants. On the Day of resurrection you will certainly not be asked, 'Why did you not curse so and so? Why were you silent about him?' On the contrary, even if throughout your life you have never cursed Iblīs and never employed your tongue in mentioning him, you will not be questioned about that or asked to give an account on the Day of Resurrection; but if you cursed anyone whom God created, you will have to give an account. Never blame anything that God most high created. The prophet (peace be upon him) would never criticize bad food when he wanted anything, he ate it; otherwise he left it alone.

7. Supplicating against people

Guard your tongue from invoking evil on anyone whom God most high has created. Even if he has wronged you, yet the whole matter is in the hands of God most high. A hadith says: 'the person oppressed will supplicate against his oppressor until he is compensated and he will have to give account on the Day of Resurrection. A certain man said much against al-Ḥajjāj, whereupon one of the salaf marked; 'As surely as God will take vengeance on al-Ḥajjāj for those he wronged, He will also take vengeance for al-Ḥajjāj on those who attack him with their tongue.

8. Jesting, ridiculing and mocking others

Guard your tongue from that, whether in earnest or in play. It disturbs your reputation; as water in a pool is disturbed by a stone, it destroys respect, induces isolation (or unsociability), and harms the heart. It is the source of disobedience, anger and discord, and implants hatred in men's hearts. Do not make fun of anyone, even if they try to associate you in their jests; do not reply to them but turn away from them until they talk about something else. Be one of those who, if they pass some idle jokes they pass on with dignity.

These are the various defects of the tongue. Nothing helps you against it except being alone and the adherence to silence wherever possible. Abu Bakr the Upright (may God be pleased with him) used to place a stone in his mouth to prevent himself speaking except when necessary; he used to point to his tongue and say, 'This is what has brought all my troubles upon me.' Guard against it, for it is the chief cause of your destruction in this world and the next.

The stomach is to be guarded from consuming anything that is unlawful or of doubtful. Try to obtain what is lawful, and when you have found it try to take less than your fill of it. Over indulging with food hardens the heart (that is, makes the mind less receptive), impairs the intellect, and weakens the memory; it makes the limbs too heavy for piety and for knowledge; it strengthens the desires and aids the hosts of Satan. To satisfy oneself to the full arising from things lawful is the source of all evil; what then of satiety from things unlawful? Likewise to look for lawful food is a duty for every Muslim. Piety and knowledge, along with eating what is unlawful, is like building on a heap of manure. If you are content with a coarse shirt throughout the year, (or 'with one coarse shirt a year'), and coarse bread rolls in twenty-four hours, and give up delighting in the finest of delicacies, then you will never lack a sufficiency of what is lawful (*halal*).

What is lawful is of many kinds. You are not required to be certain about the inner nature of things, but you must avoid what you know to be unlawful, or think to be so or the basis of some sign which is actually present and which by analogy implies unlawfulness. Now the things known to be unlawful are obvious: what is assumed to be unlawful (haram) go by the signs are: the property of the ruler and his deputies (or provincial governors), and the property of those who have no means of livelihood except (professionally) mourning for the dead or selling wine or practising usury or the playing of flutes or other instruments of pleasure. The unlawful includes even the property of the man of whom you know that the major part of his wealth is quite unlawful; while it is exceptionally possible in such a case that the actual things you receive are lawful (that is, lawfully come by), yet they must be regarded as unlawful, since that is more probable (that they are unlawfully come by). Absolutely unlawful too, is the consuming of any trust fund where that is done not in accordance with the provision of the person who made the endowment. Thus for example, what a person not engaged in theological studies receives from the trust funds of the theology schools is unlawful; and if a person has committed a sin invalidating his giving evidence, what he receives as a Sufi from a trust fund or other source is unlawful. We have dealt with the bases of the doubtful, the lawful and the unlawful in a special book of The Revival of the Religious Sciences (Book 14). You must seek it (the lawful) then; for to know and seek the lawful is obligatory for every Muslim, just like the five ṣalāts.

The private parts should be guarded from everything which God most high has made unlawful. Be as God most high said (Q. 23:5f.): '(Fortunate are . . .) those who guard their private parts, except in regard to their spouses and what their right hands possess (slave women), for they are not to be blamed'. You will not manage, however, to guard your genitals except by guarding your eyes from looking and by guarding your heart from thinking and by guarding your stomach from what is doubtful and from over indulgence, for these are the movers of desire and its seed-bed.

The (two) hands should be guarded from beating a Muslim, from receiving unlawful wealth, from harming any creature, from betraying a trust or deposit, from writing what may not be uttered—for the pen is one of man's two tongues, so guard it from the same things as the tongue. The (two) feet should be guarded from going to an unlawful place and from hastening to the court of a wicked ruler. To go to wicked rulers where there is no necessity nor compulsion is a grave sin, for it means humbling oneself before them and honouring them in their sinfulness, and God most high has commanded us to keep away from them when He said (Q. 11:113): 'And incline not towards those who do wrong, lest the Fire touch you . . .' to the end of the verse. If you do so, seeking their wealth, that is, to hasten to what is unlawful. The Prophet (peace be upon him) has said: 'When a man humbles himself before an upright rich man, two thirds of his religion goes away'. That is in the case of a rich man who is upright; what then, do you think, with a rich man who is wicked?

In general, when your bodily organs move and are at rest, these acts are some of the graces of God most high to you. Do not move any of your limbs at all in disobedience to God most high, but employ them in obeying Him. If you fall short, the evil consequences will come back upon yourself; if you are diligent, the fruits of your activity will come back to yourself. God is rich enough to do without you and your work. It is only 'by every soul will be (held) in pledge for its deeds' (Q. 74:38) (that is, men's eternal destiny depends on their conduct in this life). Beware of saying, 'God is generous and merciful; He pardons the sins of the disobedient.' This is a true word, but what is meant by it in such a context is false, and the person who repeats it is to be dubbed a fool, according to the definition of the Messenger of God (Peace be upon him) when he said: 'The shrewd man is he who masters (or abases) himself and works for what is after death; the fool is the man who makes himself follow his passions and desires things contrary to the command of God'. If you say such a thing, you clearly resemble the man who wants to be learned in the sciences of religion but spends his time in idleness and says, 'God is generous and merciful, able to fill my heart with that Knowledge with which He filled the heart of His prophets and saints, without any effort on my part, any repetition, any learning from a teacher.' Again, you resemble the man who wants wealth, yet does not engage in farming or commerce or any gainful occupation, but has no employment, and says, 'God is generous and merciful; "His are the treasures of the heavens and the earth" (Q. 63:7); He is able to make me independent of gaining a living; He has in fact done that for some men.'

Now you, on hearing what these two men say, count them fools and scoff at them, even though their description of the power and generosity of God most high is true and correct. In exactly the same way men of insight in religion laugh at you when you try to obtain forgiveness without making any effort for it. God most high says (Q. 53:40): '(Has he been told) that man will certainly see the result of his labour? and again (Q. 52:16): 'ye are only being recompensed for what ye have been doing;' and again (Q. 82:13-14): 'As for the righteous, they will be in bliss, and verily the wicked will be in a hot place.' So, if you do not, in reliance on His generosity, give up all effort to get knowledge and wealth, likewise do not give up making provision for the world to come and do not become negligent. The Lord of this world and of the next is one, and in both He is generous and merciful; His generosity does not increase through your obedience, but it consists in His making easy for you the way by which you arrive at the enduring and eternal realm through patience in setting desires aside for a few days. Such is His great generosity. Do not repeat to yourself these stupidities of the idlers, but imitate men of prudence and resolution, the prophets and the righteous. Do not long to reap what you did not sow. Would that all who fasted and performed the prayer and engaged in the struggle and were pious had been forgiven!

These are all the things from which you must guard your external organs. The acts of these organs develop only through the attributes of the heart. If, then, you want to guard your organs, you must purify your heart, that is, be inwardly pious and not merely outwardly. The heart is the 'morsel of flesh'. (Q. 22:5; 23:14; second stage of the embryo) whose soundness leads to the soundness of the whole body; so see to its soundness in order that thereby your organs may be sound.

9. The Sins of the Heart

The blameworthy qualities in the heart are many, the purification of the heart from its defects is lengthy, and the means of treating these is obscure. People are so lacking in concern for themselves and so their fascination with the worlds glamour and glitter that the knowledge and practice of that treatment have altogether disappeared. We have dealt fully with all that in our work on The Revival of the Religious Sciences, in the parts about 'Destructive acts and acts of salvation', (the third and fourth 'quarters'); but here we warn you against three of the evil dispositions of the heart—the most prominent among the religious scholars of our time—so that you may be on your guard against them; for they are both destructive in themselves and the roots of all other evil dispositions. They are envy, hypocrisy and pride (or self-admiration). Endeavour to purify your heart from them. If you master these, you know how to guard against the others mentioned among the things destructive; if you are unable to deal with them, you will be all the more unable to deal with others. Do not imagine that you will preserve a sound intention in your pursuit of learning while there is any envy, hypocrisy or pride in your heart.

The Prophet (peace be upon him) said; 'Three things are destructive: greed, desires given rein to, and admiration of oneself.

A. Envy

This is a form of greed, for the miser is the man who is mean towards others with his possession; the greedy person is the one who is selfish towards the servants of God most high with God's blessings where that is in the treasure chest of His might and not in his own treasuries—so his greed is greater. The envious man is the one who is pained when God most high out of the treasuries of His might bestows on one of His servants knowledge or wealth or popularity or some piece of good fortune, and who therefore wants that favour taken away from the other person, even though he himself will not obtain any advantage from its removal. This is the depths of evil.

Hence the Messenger of God (peace be upon him) said: 'Envy eats up good deeds as fire eats up wood.' The envious man suffers punishment and receives no mercy. He is continually suffering punishment in this world, for the world never lacks among his contemporaries and acquaintances many on whom God has bestowed knowledge or wealth or influence, and thus he continually suffers punishment in this world until his death. And the punishment of the world to come is even greater and more severe. Indeed a man does not arrive at true faith so long as he does not want for the rest of the Muslims what he wants for himself. Indeed, he must be equal to them in prosperity and adversity. The Muslims are like a single building, one part of which supports the other; they are like a single body, in which, if one part suffers, the rest of the body is affected. If you do not find this state of affairs in your heart, then it is more important for you to busy yourself with seeking deliverance from destruction than to busy yourself with fiqhi questions of issues of disagreement.

B. Hypocrisy

This is hidden polytheism (*shirk*), one of the two forms of polytheism (associating partners with God). It consists of seeking a place in the hearts of people that you thereby obtain adoration and respect. The love of influence is one of the 'desires given rein to', and through it many people go to destruction. Yet people are destroyed only by themselves. If people really judged objectively, they would realise that it is only people's hypocrisy which is the motive of most of their intellectual pursuits and acts of Worship, not to mention their customary activities; and his hypocrisy renders their acts of no avail. Thus we find in Tradition, 'On the Day of Resurrection orders will be given to take the martyr to the Fire, and he will say, "O Lord, I was martyred fighting in Your path," and God most high will say to him, "You wanted it to be known that so and so is brave; that has been conveyed, and therefore that is your reward." The same will be said of the scholar, the man who has performed the pilgrimage to Makkah, and the reciter of the Quran (*qari*).

C. Pride, arrogance, boastfulness

This is the chronic disease. It is man's consideration to see himself with the eye of self-glorification and self-importance and his consideration to see others with the eye of contempt. The result as regards the tongue is that he says, 'I. I. . .' as accursed Iblis said (Q. 38:77): 'I am better than he; You have created me of fire, but him You have created of clay'. The fruit of it in society is self-promotion and self-advancement and to seek priority to speak first in gatherings and resentment when what one says is contradicted. The arrogant man is he who, when he gives advice, he is tough, but, when he receives it, is rude.

Everyone who considers himself better than one of the creatures of God most high is arrogant. Indeed, you ought to realise that the good man in the sight of God is he who is good with respect to the hereafter and the hereafter is something unseen by man, and it all depends on how his ending was. Your belief that you are better than others is sheer ignorance. Rather you ought not to look at anyone without considering that he is better than you and superior to you. Thus, if you see a child, you say, 'This person has never sinned against God, but I have sinned, and so he is better than I;' and if you see an older person, you say, 'This man was a servant of God before me, and is certainly better than I;' if he is a scholar you say, 'This man has been given what I have not been given and reached what I did not reach, and knows what I am ignorant of; then how shall I be like him?' and if he is ignorant, you say, 'This man has sinned against God in ignorance, and I have sinned against Him knowingly, so God's case against me is stronger, and I do not know what end He will give to me and what end to him'; if he is an infidel, you say, 'I do not know; perhaps he will become a Muslim and his life will end in doing good, and because of his acceptance of Islam something of his sins will be taken away, as a strand of hair is removed from dough; but as for me—God is our refuge (God grant it does not happen)—perhaps God will let me stray so that I disbelieve and my life ends in doing evil, and then tomorrow he will be among those brought near to God and I shall be among the punished.'

Arrogance will not leave your heart except when you know that the great man is he who is great in the sight of God most high. That is something which cannot be known until the end of life, and there is doubt about that (the end and whether it will be good or bad). So you should be preoccupied with the fear of an impious end (of life) accompanied by uncertainty, to show arrogance towards the servants of God the most high. Your certitude and faith at present do not exclude the possibility of your changing in the future; for God is the disposer of hearts; He guides whom He will and leads astray whom He will.

The Traditions (*ahadith*) about envy, arrogance, hypocrisy and pride are numerous. A single comprehensive tradition about them will suffice you. Ibn al-Mubārak related, with a chain of authorities going back to a certain man, that this man said to Mu'ādh, 'O Mu'ādh, tell me a Tradition you heard from the Messenger of God (peace be upon him).' The man continued: 'Mu'ādh wept until I thought he would never cease, but at length he ceased; then he said: 'I heard the Messenger of God (peace be upon him) saying to me: 'I am going to tell you a Tradition (or tell you of a happening), Mu'ādh; if you memorise it, it will benefit you before God, but if you forget it and do not remember it, your plea of defence before God on the Day of Resurrection will be removed. O Mu'ādh, God (most high and glorified) created seven angels before creating the heavens and the earth, and to each of the heavens He appointed one of these seven angels as keeper. Now the guardian angels are ascending carrying man's deeds from morning to evening; and the deeds seem to glow like that of the sun. When they bring it up to the lowest heaven, they increase and multiply it, and the angel at the gate says to the guardians, "With this deed strike the face of the doer of it; I am in charge of backbiting; my Lord has commanded me not to allow the deed of anyone guilty of backbiting to pass beyond me.' He continued: 'Then the guardians bring one of man's good deeds and increase and multiply it, until they reach the second heaven with it. The angel responsible for it says "Stand and with this deed strike the face of the doer of it, for in his work he sought worldly honour; my Lord has commanded me not to allow his deed to pass beyond me; he boasted in men's society of his superiority; I am the angel dealing with boastfulness." He continued: 'The guardians ascend with a man's deeds, so bright with light from alms, prayer and fasting that the guardians were astonished.

They passed with it to the third heaven, and there the angel in charge says to them, "Stand and with this deed strike the face of the doer of it; I am the angel dealing with arrogance; my Lord has commanded me not to let his deed pass beyond me for he has treated people arrogantly in society." He continued: 'The guardians ascent with a man's deeds shining brightly like a star and ringing from the acts of adoration and prayer, from fasting and from the greater and lesser pilgrimages, until they pass with it to the fourth heaven. Then the angel responsible for that says to them, "Stand and with this deed strike the face and back and front of the doer of this work; I am in charge of pride; my Lord has commanded me not to let this act pass beyond me; whenever this man performed any deed, pride entered into it." He continued: 'The guardians ascend with a man's deeds and pass with it to the fifth heaven; it is like a bride being taken to her husband. The angel responsible for it says to the guardians, "Stand and with this deed strike the face of the doer of it, and carry them away and place him on his shoulder; I am the angel dealing with envy; this man used to envy whoever studied and performed a deed like his and all who were superior to men in some way; he used to envy them and slander them; my Lord has commanded me not to allow his deed to pass beyond me.— He continued: 'The guardians ascend with a man's deeds, radiant as the moon from prayer and almsgiving and the greater and lesser pilgrimages and the holy war (jihad) and fasting, and they pass with it to the sixth heaven, where the angel responsible for that says to them, "Stand and with this deed strike the face of the doer of it; he never had mercy on any of God's servants who had met with misfortune or sickness, but rejoiced at that; I am the angel of mercy; my Lord commanded me not to allow his deed to pass beyond me." He continued: 'The guardians ascend with a man's deed consisting of prayer and fasting and the spending of money (in good causes, or otherwise as alms) and the holy war (*jihad*) and his cautiousness (from falling into haram); it had a sound like that of bees and a radiance like that of the sun; along with it were three thousand angels and they passed with it to the seventh heaven. The angel responsible for that said to them, "Stand and with that deed strike the face of the doer of it and with it strike his limbs and lock up his heart; I veil from my Lord every deed that is not done for the sake of my Lord; this deed was done for the sake of something other than God most high; he did it for the sake of honour among the religious scholars ('ulamā) and fame among the intellectuals and renown among the cities; my Lord commanded me not to allow his work to pass beyond me; every work not done purely for God is hypocrisy, and God does not receive the work of the hypocrite." He continued: 'The guardians ascend with a man's deed consisting of prayer, almsgiving, fasting, the greater and lesser pilgrimages, a good character, observance of silence and remembrance of God most high. It is accompanied by the angels of the seven heavens until they have passed through all the veils to the presence of God most high. Then they stand before Him and bear witness to Him of the good deed, performed solely for the sake of God most high; and God most high says, 'you are the guardians over the work of My servant, but I am the Watcher over his heart; this act was not done for My sake, but for the sake of something else; so My curse is upon him." Then the angels all say, "Thy curse and our curse be upon him;" and the seven heavens and those in them curse him. At that Muādh wept, and then continued: "I said: O Messenger of God, you are the Messenger of God, and I am Mu'ādh; how shall I have purity of intention and salvation?' The Messenger of God (Peace be upon him) said: 'Imitate me, even if you fall short somewhat in what you do. O Mu'ādh, guard your tongue from slandering your brothers who know the Quran by heart, attribute your sins to yourself and not to them; do not justify yourself and blame them; do not exalt yourself above them; do not mingle the work of this world with the work of the world to come; do not act arrogantly in society so that men avoid you because of your bad character; do not whisper to one man while another is also present; do not magnify your importance above other men so that you lose the good things of both this world and the world to come; do not tear to pieces people's characters so that on the Day of Resurrection the dogs of Hell tear you to pieces in Hell. God most high says (Q. 79:2); "By those who draw forth;" do you know what these are, O Mu'ādh?' I said: 'What are they, O Messenger of God (may you be ransomed by my father and mother)?' He said: 'The dogs in Hell drawing the flesh from the bones.' I said: O Messenger of God (may you be ransomed by my father and mother) who is able to acquire these good qualities, and who will escape from these dogs'?' He said: O Mu'ādh, it is indeed easy for him for whom God makes it easy.'

Khālid b. Mi'dān said: 'I never saw anyone showing more care and perseverance in reading the noble Quran than Mu'ādh on account of this noble Tradition'.

So, you who desire knowledge, reflect on these (bad) qualities. Undoubtedly the greatest cause of these vices becoming established in the heart is the pursuit of knowledge in order to dispute with others and outshine them. The ordinary man is far removed from these bad qualities, but the scholar or theologian is in the way of them and is exposed to destruction because of them. Consider, then, which of your affairs is most important—to learn how to guard against these 'things destructive' and to occupy yourself with the improvement of your heart and the preparation of your eternal life or whether it is more important to engage along with the others in the pursuit of such knowledge as will increase your arrogance, hypocrisy, envy and pride, until along with the others you perish.

Undoubtedly, these three qualities are the roots of the vices of the heart, and they have a one main outcome, namely, the love of this world. For that reason the Messenger of God (peace be upon him) said, 'The love of this world is the source of all sin'. At the same time, this world is a field sown for (reaping in) the world to come. If a man takes from this world only as much as is necessary, to help him with regard to the world to come, then this world is for him a field that has been sown; but if he wants this world to enjoy it, then this world is his place of downfall.

The above is a small part of the science of piety in its exterior aspects and it is the Beginning of Guidance. If you try it out on yourself in practice and find it acceptable to you, then you must turn to The Revival of the Religious Sciences and become acquainted with piety in its interior aspect. When you have built up the interior of your heart in piety (*taqwa*), at that the veils between you and your Lord will be removed, the light of spiritual knowledge will be revealed to you, there will burst forth from your heart the springs of wisdom, and the secrets of the worldly realm will be made clear to you. Such sciences will become familiar to you that you will hold of no account these innovative sciences which did not exist in the days of the Companions (may God be pleased with them) and their successors. If, however, you pursue the science of argument and counter-argument, of contradiction and dispute the witness, how great will be your misfortune, how prolonged will be your efforts and how great will be your disappointment and your loss! Do as you wish because this world which you seek with religiosity will not surrender to you and the hereafter will be removed from you. The man who makes his religion a means to the gaining of this world, will lose both worlds alike whereas the man who gives up this world for the sake of religion (*din*), will gain both worlds alike.

This is all the Guidance to the Beginning of the way in respect of your dealings with God most high by performing what He commands and avoiding what He forbids.

IV. RELATIONSHIP BETWEEN GOD AND MAN, AND BETWEEN MAN AND MAN

1. Companionship with God

Know that your Companion who does not leave you, whether you are residing in a place permanently or travelling, whether you are sleeping or awake, and indeed whether you are alive or dead, is in fact your Guardian, your Master, and your Creator. Whenever you remember Him He is there, as He most high said, 'I am the Companion of him who remembers Me,'

When your mind is filled with grief over your shortcomings in your duties, God is your inseparable Companion, as God most high said, 'I am with those whose minds are filled with grief for My sake.'

If you knew God truly and perfectly, you would take Him for a Companion and leave people aside. Should you be unable to do this all the time, take care that your day and night are not without a time in which you will be alone with your Master and enjoy the pleasure of your secret conversation with Him. For that you have to learn and follow the rules of companionship with Him most high.

The rules are: keeping silent with the head cast down, ignoring [one's surroundings] and concentrating on God, continuance of silence, stillness of the limbs, yearning to carry out His commands and avoiding His prohibitions, not complaining against fate, continual remembrance of God and reflection on His [majesty] prefer truth over falsehood, independence from people, humility before the awe of Him, a sense of shame, peace of mind from the worries of earning a livelihood while relying on the guarantee of sustenance by God, and trust in the bounty of God knowing that He chooses for man only that which is good for him.

All these should be your distinctive characteristics in all your days and nights, for they are the rules of companionship with a Companion Who does not leave you [at all], whereas [your companions from among] people sometimes leave you.

2. Companionship and Association with People
A. Etiquettes of the scholar
If you are a learned man you should observe the rules of a man of knowledge which are seventeen in number: [1] patience, [2] continual forbearance, [3] when seated, to sit in a dignified manner with the head cast down, [4] not to take pride at the expense of anyone except oppressors as deterrent to their oppression, [5] show humility in assemblies, [6] not to jest and joke, [7] kindness towards students, [8] to act unhurriedly with those who are proud [9] correction of the dull judiciously without being impatient, [10] not to be too vain to confess one's own ignorance of a problem, [11] to give full attention to one who asks questions and to try to understand them, [12] acceptance of preponderant evidence in an argument, [13] to yield to the truth by turning towards it from error, [14] to forbid the student any knowledge which is harmful to him, [15] to prevent him from seeking other than God's pleasure while seeking beneficial knowledge, [16] to keep the student from occupying himself with 'communal obligation' before completing the 'individual obligation', his 'individual obligation' being the correction of his outward (ẓāhir) and inward (bāṭin) self with piety (taqwā), and [17] the correction of himself with piety first so that his student may follow him first through his examples and then his words.

B. Etiquettes of the student

If you are a student you should observe the praiseworthy rules of a student's dealing with a learned man. These rules are: to greet the learned man first, to speak little in his presence, not to speak unless first asked by the teacher, not to ask him questions before taking his permission, not to contradict the teacher by saying 'so-and-so said contrary to what you have said', not to argue whisper to another student in his gatherings, not to look around but to sit quietly and courteously as if you were engaged in a ritual prayer, not to speak to him much when he is tired, to stand up in order to show respect for him when he stands, not to follow him speaking and asking him questions on the way until he reaches his home, not to form bad impression of him in regard to those of his actions which may appear abominable. The teacher knows better concerning his secret affairs.

When some actions of the teacher appear abominable, the student should recall the complaint made by the prophet Musa to Khiḍir (may peace be upon them both), 'Have you made a hole in the boat to drown the people in it? You have, indeed, done a strange thing!' In fact Musa was wrong in his complaint which he made relying upon the outward appearance of what Khiḍir did.

C. Etiquettes of the child (with parent)

If your parents are alive you should observe the manners of a child with his parents. These rules are: to listen to what the parents say, to stand up in order to show respect to them when they stand, to obey their orders, not to walk ahead of them, not to raise your voice over their voices, to answer to their call, earnestly to desire to please them, to be humbly tender with them, not to remind them of any good thing done for them or undertaken a service, not to look at them irritatedly, not to frown in their faces, and not to travel [to a distant place] without their permission.

D. Etiquettes with unknown people

Know that besides teachers, students and parents, people are of three kinds. They are either your friends, acquaintances, and those not known to you. If you are involved with people whom you do not know, you should observe the rules of sitting in their company. They are: to avoid engaging in conversation with them, not paying too much attention to the news and rumours they may be spreading, to ignore and disregard any bad words they habitually utter, to guard against meeting them frequently and against being in need of them, to gently bring to their attention what is distasteful and admonish them when there is hope that they may accept the admonition.

E. Etiquettes with friends

Concerning your brethren and friends, you have two tasks:

[1]. You should first consider the demands and obligations of friendship so that you will establish the relationship of brotherhood only with those who are fit for brotherhood and friendship. The Messenger of God (may god bless him and greet him) said, 'A man is upon the religion of his intimate friend (*khalil*); so let each of you consider whom he has taken for an intimate friend.

When you try to find a companion in order that he may be your partner in the acquisition of knowledge and in matters of religious and worldly pursuits, look for five qualities in him.

The first quality is intelligence. There is no good in the companionship of a stupid man. Companionship with such a man results in isolation and separation. He will end up doing harm to you when he really intends to help you. An intelligent enemy is better than a stupid friend. As 'Ali (may God be pleased with him) said:

> Do not be in the company of an ignorant;
> Beware of him and let him beware of you.

> How often an ignorant man has brought ruin
> To a forbearing man when befriended
> A man is measured by his companion
> When that man walks with him.
> Like the similarity of one shoe to another
> When it is set opposite to it.
> Estimation and comparisons are made to evaluate
> A soul evaluates another soul which it encounters.

The second quality [of a prospective friend] is good character. Do not be the companion of a man who is unable to control himself when he is angry and is excited when he desires something. 'Alqamah al-'Uṭārdī (may God have mercy upon him) gathered good characteristics in his counsel which he gave to his son at the time of his death. He said in that will,

> Dear son, when you want the companionship of a man, be the companion of him who will protect you when you employ him in your service, will adorn you if you are his companion, and if you are in financial need he will assist you. Be the companion of him who will extend his helping hand to you when you extend to him your hand for help, will acknowledge it a good thing if he sees something good proceeding from you, but will stop an evil if he sees it being done by you. Be the companion of a man who will consider you truthful when you speak, will assist you and help you if you desire anything and try for it, and will give preference to your view if you both dispute on any matter.

'Ali (may God be pleased with him) said in a poem, Your true friend is he who is always with you, And he will suffer himself in order to benefit you, And he who, when calamities of the time break you, scatters his cloak in order to save you.

The third quality [of a prospective friend] is piety. Do not be the companion of a wicked man (fasiq) who persists in major sins. This is because he who fears God does not persist in any major sin, and he who does not fear God may cause you mischief; indeed, his attitude towards you will change with the changes in his fortune and conditions. God (most high) commanded his Prophet (may God bless him and greet him), 'Do not yield to those whose hearts We have allowed to be neglectful of the remembrance of Us and who follows his own passions, and whose case exceeds all bounds.' (Q. 18:20).

Beware, then, of associating with a wicked man, because the continual disobedience to God will remove the dislike of sin from your mind and will create the feeling that sin is something light. The sinfulness of backbiting has become light to man's mind for this reason and not for the reason that the mind cannot understand it. If people see that a Muslim jurist (*faqih*) is wearing a gold ring or silkcloth, they would strongly rebuke it because they rarely see this, however they tolerate backbiting even though it is a more serious sin, because their familiarity with backbiting.

The fourth quality [of a prospective friend] is absence of greed. Do not be the companion of a greedy man. Companionship of a man greedy for the world is deadly poison, for human nature is such that the character of one man tends to influence that of another without him being aware of it. Therefore, association with a greedy man will increase your greed, and association with the ascetics will increase you in yoiur renunciation of this world.

The fifth quality [of a prospective friend] is truthfulness. Do not be the companion of a liar, for he is like the mirage: he will make the distant (object) look near and that which is near remote from you.

Perhaps it's possible these five qualities do not exist in a single person residing in academic institutions and mosques [i.e.

the intellectuals and the devotees]. You must therefore do one of two things. Either you adopt solitude and loneliness, for in it lies your safety. Or you live in society, but your association with your fellow-men will be in proportion to their qualities. You must know that brotherhood is of three kinds—[1] a brother who is good for your Hereafter, so that you will observe in him only the religious quality; [2] a brother is for your good in this world, so that you will observe in him only good character; and [3] a brother who is only a sociable companion, so that you must avoid his evil, mischief and wickedness.

Men are of three categories. The first group is like nourishment, no one can exist without it. Another is like medicine which is needed from time to time but not always. A third man is like a disease which is never needed but with which man is sometimes afflicted. The last one is he in whom there is neither good company nor benefit. Kind treatment of him is necessary so as to escape from him. In seeing him, there is a great benefit provided you are helped by God to obtain it. The benefit is that you perceive some of his wickedness and bad deeds and so you avoid them. Fortunate is he who is warned by others; a believer in God (al-mu'min) is like a mirror of another believer. Someone asked Jesus Christ (Peace be upon him), 'Who has taught you courtesy?' He replied, 'None. Rather I saw the ignorance of the ignorant and so avoided it.' Jesus (may God bless and greet him as well as our Prophet!) has indeed spoken the truth. If people were to avoid whatever they considered evil in others, they would possess perfect courtesy and need no one to instruct them in it.

[2]. Your second task concerning your brethren and friends is to fulfil the duties of friendship and close companionship. When friendship is established and companionship between your friend and you exists, certain duties become incumbent upon you. In carrying out these duties, certain rules have to be followed. The Prophet (Peace be upon him) said, 'Two persons

who have become brethren by the acceptance of Islam are like two hands washing each other.'

The Prophet (Peace be upon him) once entered a thicket (dense bush) and picked up two tooth-sticks (miswak), one of which was crooked and the other straight. He gave the straight one to a certain companion of his who was with him and kept the crooked one for himself. His companion said, 'Messenger of God, you deserve the straight one more than I.' The Prophet (Peace be upon him) replied, 'Anyone who becomes the companion of another, even for only an hour of the day, will most certainly be asked [on the Day of Judgement] as to whether, in his companionship, he has fulfilled or neglected the duties set by God.'

The Prophet (Peace be upon him) further said, Of two persons who keep company with each other, the more beloved to God (exalted be He) is certainly he who is more kind to his companion.'

The duties of friendship are:

1. To help the friend financially even when one's own needs are not satisfied. If this altruism is not possible, one should help the friend with one's surplus wealth at the time of his need. One should also assist him in his needs spontaneously, before he seeks assistance.

2. To hide his secrets, and to conceal his faults.

3. Not to convey to him others' disdain for him thereby making him unhappy. Rather to convey to him others' praise of him, thereby pleasing him.

4. To listen to him with full attention when he speaks and not to argue with him.

5. To call him with that name which he likes most, to praise him by mentioning his deeds that one knows, and to express gratitude to him in his presence for the good deeds he has done.

6. To defend the friend in his absence when there is an attack on his integrity, as one defends oneself.

7. To admonish him with kindness and in ambiguous terms when he needs admonition.

8. To forgive his faults and errors and not to blame him.

9. In one's solitude, to pray for the friend during his lifetime and also after his death.

10. To take care of a friend's wife and his other relatives after his death.

11. To choose to make things easy for the friend; so one will not burden him with the meeting of any of one's needs.

12. To give rest to his mind by removing causes of distress.

13. To express joy at all his delights, and to express sorrow at all untoward things which happen to him, and to keep in mind that feeling for him which has been expressed to him so that one become truthful in one's friendship, both secretly and openly.

14. To greet the friend first when he approaches, to make room for him, to come out from the house to receive him, to see him off when he leaves, to keep silent when he speaks until he completes his conversation, and not to interrupt him when speaking. In short, one is to behave with one's friend

just as one would like him to behave with you. The brotherhood [i.e., friendship] of a man who does not want for his brother what he wants for himself is hypocrisy (nifāq), and is an evil for him in this world and the Hereafter.

The above are the rules you have to follow when dealing with ordinary men who are unknown to you and with friends taken as brothers.

3. Association with acquaintances

Beware of your acquaintances, for you will receive only evil from those whom you do not know intimately. Your friends will render help to you, those who are completely unknown to you will not harm you, but evil will come upon you through those acquaintances who only express friendship with their tongues. So reduce the number of such acquaintances as far as possible.

When you are associated with acquaintances in an academic institution, or big or small mosque, or town, or market, you must not despise any one of them, for you do not know, perhaps he is better than you.

Do not treat them great seeing their well-to-do worldly standing, lest you be destroyed: because the world has little worth in the estimation of God, and all that is in it is also of little value; so whenever worldly men appear to be great in your mind, you fall away from the eyes of God (exalted be He). Guard yourself against using your religion in order to gain some of their worldly possessions. Anyone who did this would become low in their eyes and would fail to get their possessions.

If your acquaintances are hostile to you do not reply with enmity, for you are unable to be content when they retaliate; so your religious nature will disappear in their enmity towards you; thus your difficulties with them will be prolonged. [On the other hand], if they respect you, praise you in your presence and express their friendship for you, do not trust them, for if you enquire into the real nature of this you will not find even one percent of them sincere in their behaviour. Do not expect that their behaviour will be the one and the same in public and in private. Do not be astonished if they rebuke you in your absence and do not be angry for that, because, should you be fair, you would find similar behaviour in yourself even concerning your friends and relatives, and indeed concerning your teachers and parents—in their absence you talk of things concerning them which you will not mention in their presence

Completely abandon your greed for wealth, influence and assistance from your acquaintances. A greedy man usually becomes loser in the future and is necessarily humiliated in the present. If you ask anyone of them to satisfy your needs and he does so, be grateful to God as well as to him; if, however, he falls short, do not blame him and do not complain against him [to anyone], lest enmity arise between him and you. Be like a believer in God (al-mu'min) who seeks to find excuses for people, and do not be like a hypocrite who seeks to find fault; console yourself by saying, 'Perhaps the man fell short of satisfying my need for a reason which I do not know.'

Do not offer your opinion on any matter to an acquaintance unless you first perceive an indication of his acceptance; otherwise he will not listen to you but will reject you. If, however, he had made a mistake and the mistake had led him to the commission of a sin, tell him the truth with kindness, not with roughness.

When you see that your acquaintances respect you and do good to you, be grateful to God Who has made you beloved to them. But if you find them doing evil to you, entrust them to God, seek the protection of Him (exalted be He) against their evil, do not reproach them, and do not say. 'Why do you not recognise my right seeing that I am so-and-so, the son of so-and-so, and seeing that I am a learned man?' Do not say this because it is the stupid men who say this. The most stupid man is he who ascribes purity to himself and praises himself. Know that God gives them power over you [do that they do evil to you] only for sins you have committed. So seek forgiveness of God for your sins. Know that God only granted them some authority over you because of your sins so seek forgiveness over your sin and realise that it was a penalty from God to you. Beware of association with the learned men of this time, especially those who busy themselves with the differences of opinions and intellectual disputes. Beware of them; because of their jealousy they wait for you to fall into ill-fortune, imagine various things concerning you, and behind your back make signs with their eyes (winking) among themselves while mentioning each of your faults when they meet together so that sometimes in their anger they confront you with these faults or slips; nor do they hide your private matters which should be kept hidden. They make an account with you even in the most negligible matter, and they envy you in everything, small or great. They instigate your friends against you by slandering, spreading false information, and lies. If they are pleased with you they show it through excessive flattery; if they are angry with you they display their bitterness. On their bodies they wear beautiful clothes, but their minds are wolves. This is a judgment based on clear observations of most of them except those whom God (exalted is He!) has protected. Companionship with them is a loss, and association with them is to be forsaken. If the above is the judgement on those who express their friendship to you, how grave will be the judgement on those who openly declared their enmity towards you?

Al-Qāḍī ibn Ma'rū f (may God bestow mercy upon him!) said:
   Beware of your enemy once,
   But beware of your friend a thousand times,
   For a friend turns to be an enemy sometimes,
   And then knows better how to harm you.

In the same vein Abu Tamām said:
> Your enemy sometimes comes from your friend,
> So do not increase the number of friends;
> Most of the diseases that you see,
> Originate from eating and drinking.

Be as Hilāl ibn al-'Alā' said:
> When I forgave and bore no rancour to anyone,
> I gave rest to myself from anxiety about enemies.
> I greet my enemy when I see him,
> That I may repel evil by greetings.
> I express cheerfulness to a man I hate,
> As if he has filled my mind with delights.
> I am not safe from those whom I do not know,
> So how can I be safe from those who are friends?
> Men are a disease and the only remedy is forsaking them,
> By being harsh with them we cut off brotherhood.
> Then keep men at a safe distance and you will be safe from their mischiefs,
> And be earnestly desirous of requiring friendship.
> And behave well with men and endure what comes from them;
> Be deaf, dumb, blind and one who is God-fearing.

Also, as a certain wise man admonished, 'Meet your friend and your enemy with a pleasing smile, without lowering oneself and without fear of them; and be dignified without pride, be humble without lowering oneself.' In all your affairs be moderate; extremes in all affairs are blameworthy, as a certain poet said:
> You must be moderate in all affairs,
> For this is a straight path to the plain road;
> Do not be excessive or deficient concerning anything,
> For both states of affairs are blameworthy

THE BEGINNING OF GUIDANCE

Do not look in pride to the left and to the right and do not look around much. Do not stand beside a group of men, but sit with them; and when you sit, do not sit so as to be ready to rise. Be on your guard against fiddling with your fingers, playing with your beard and your rings, picking the teeth, inserting your fingers into your nostrils, spitting a lot, blowing or wiping your nose, driving flies away from your face, spreading the arms about while walking, yawning in the faces of people, or in prayer. Let your meetings be a guide to the truth and your talk be orderly arranged. Listen to good talk from those who speak to you, without expressing excessive surprise, and do not ask them to repeat it. Be quiet in gatherings, speak in a well thought out and organised fashion. Do not speak of your high opinion of your child, poetry, speech, books, and all other things which are special to you. Do not wear clothes designed to impress. Do not adopt a style like the style of a slave. Guard against the use of too much eye shadow and oil, and do not ask too much for help in your needs. Do not encourage or support anyone to do injustice and oppression. Do not make the amount of your wealth known to your wife or child let alone others, for if they find it small they will have contempt for you, and if they find it enormous you will never be able to please them with wealth. Be strict with them without treating them harshly, and be tender with them without weakness. Do not jest with maids or butler, lest your dignity fall. When you dispute, be patient, protect yourself from your ignorance and haste, and think of your proof. Do not hint a lot with your hands. Do not look often behind you. Do not kneel on your knees. Speak when your anger is appeased. If the ruler wants to be your acquaintance, be very wary as you would be wary of the blade of a spearhead. Beware of one who is your friend only when you are healthy and prosperous, for he is the greatest of all your enemies. Do not make your wealth more valuable than your honour. This counsel, O young man, is sufficient for you concerning the beginning of guidance. Test yourself with it. It consists of three parts. One on the rules of acts of obedience to God, one on the relationships and interactions with people. These three aspects includes all dealings of a man with the Creator and the creatures. Should you find this beginning of guidance suitable to you and your mind inclined to it and desirous of acting in accordance with it, then know that you are a man whose soul God has illuminated and broadened with faith (*iman*). Be confirmed that this beginning of guidance has a limit and that beyond it exist secrets, deep levels of understanding, wider knowledge, and disciplines and intuitions (mukāshafāt). These we have set forth in our work, The Revival of the Religious Sciences. Be occupied then with the attainment of it. If you find that your carnal desire (nafs) finds these tasks and routines too difficult and regards this kind of knowledge problematic asking you, 'How can this knowledge benefit you in the meetings of the scholars?; when will it put you in the forefront among your peers and men of reflection?; and how can it elevate your status in the assembly of princes and governors in order that it may bring you to wealth and other means of living, to the management of endowments and to the post of a judge and magistrate?,' then realise that Satan has misled you and has caused you to forget the place to which you will return and the place of dwelling after death. So seek for yourself a Satan like yourself in order that he may teach you that knowledge which, you imagine, will benefit you and bring you to what you desire. But then know that the kingdom will never be pure for you in your locality, let alone your village and town; then, on the Day of Judgement, you will miss the eternal kingdom and the everlasting delight in the near presence of the Lord of all the worlds. May peace, God's mercy and blessings be upon you! Praise be to God first and last, outwardly and inwardly! There is no ability or power except with God, the High, the Great. May God bless and greet our leader, Muhammad, and his family and his companions!

www.ingramcontent.com/pod-product-compliance
Lightning Source LLC
Chambersburg PA
CBHW012006090526
44590CB00026B/3899